D0442300

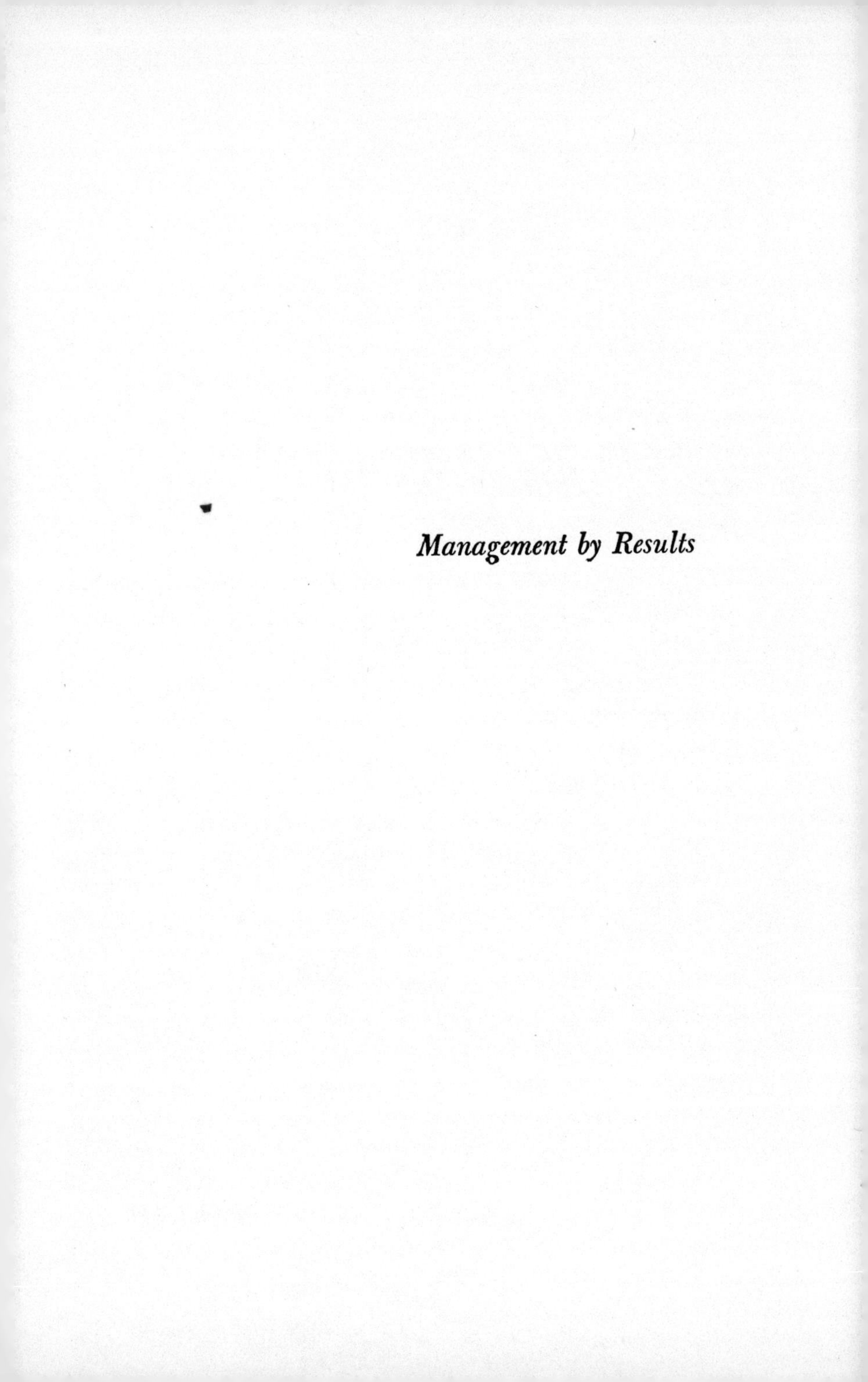

Management by Results

Management by Results

THE DYNAMICS OF
PROFITABLE MANAGEMENT

Edward C. Schleh

SCHLEH ASSOCIATES, INC.
MINNEAPOLIS, MINNESOTA

McGRAW-HILL BOOK COMPANY

New York *San Francisco* *Toronto*
London *Sydney*

MANAGEMENT BY RESULTS

Library of Congress Catalog Card Number: 61-15460

55320
9101112-VB-10987

Preface

Many books have been written on management. Some are compendia of the practices of a number of companies, while others focus on procedures that may be helpful in application. Each of these approaches has its merits. In contrast, this book attempts to present a complete and cohesive philosophy of management that could be applied to any type of enterprise at any level. Each of the principles presented is an integral part of the total philosophy and together they will, in our opinion, provide a comprehensive approach to the solving of almost any management problem. Some principles are, of course, adapted from presentations of other management thinkers. All, however, are presented as parts of a way of thinking that we call "results" management—a way of thinking that develops men to a greater accomplishment toward the long-range objectives of the enterprise.

In the early part of the book certain basic principles are presented that are applicable to the relationship between a supervisor and an employee, no matter what the level of the position. As the book progresses, these all-pervading principles are built into the more complex principles applicable to a variegated enterprise. The fundamental theme, however, is that all management must be looked at from a grass-roots approach that focuses on what must be accomplished at the bottom level of an enterprise, the place where most accomplishment actually occurs. In our opinion, this point is often lost sight of: that the major function of higher-level management and company staff is merely to make this bottom level more effective. Examples used to illustrate the principles presented are chosen rather heavily from the areas of manufacturing and sales, because these examples are apt to be understood by more people. Examples could just as well have been taken from other types of enterprise, either private or governmental.

While full responsibility for the philosophy set forth in this book must rest with the author, no philosophy ever develops without the assistance and impact of many people. I am therefore indebted to numerous clients, friends, and associates who have over the years provided the stimulus for thought and the ideas, frequently corrective, which have been gradually built into the philosophy here presented. I am especially indebted to the associates in my consulting firm for their many constructive suggestions.

Edward C. Schleh

Contents

1

The Challenge of Management

To ACCOMPLISH his objectives a manager manages men. But since each man is a thinking, feeling, unique individual, he expects a personal return or satisfaction if he is to subjugate himself to the broader direction of another. This was recognized when one man first hired another to work for him. The manager had objectives to reach for which he needed the other man. The only way he could get the help of the other man was to make such service worthwhile to him. This seems to have been readily appreciated in the personal relationship established between two men in the primary, simplified stage of management. As human institutions become more complicated, however, this personal relationship tends to be lost or changed.

The feudal system went one step beyond this primary type of organization. The main purpose was defense—

the overriding value to the people. Because conditions were chaotic, a feudal baron could force people to do many things which they might deeply resent. He could dictate jobs; there would be little recourse. It was essential that they submit to some such autocratic form of government for common defense.

As governments became more and more stable, steps were gradually taken to eliminate the power of the feudal barons. With the coming of the Industrial Revolution, businesses of various types began to replace these feudal institutions. While ostensibly the individual worker was free to come and go as he pleased and to exercise individual pressure for the satisfaction of his wants, the initial tendency was to carry over much of the feudal thinking into the operation of a business. The owner was to some extent an autocrat. Initially there was little recourse, little legal procedure to enable the employee to force the satisfaction of his own needs. Pressure was therefore exerted through legislation and through unions for a greater recognition of the desires of the individual being managed.

At the same time, however, industry was becoming more and more complex. More and more complicated machinery was being used. New ways had been developed for the harnessing of power. This led inevitably to higher speeds, to greater productivity per machine, and, concomitantly, to much greater productivity per man-hour. With the increase in speeds and power, closer tolerances were also demanded for fuller mechanization.

With the higher speeds and greater mechanization, mass markets became more imperative. More capital was needed, more technical knowledge and more research, leading to broader developments in other fields. Transportation advanced by leaps and bounds. The leap from the horse to the car—to the train—to the plane—to the jet-propelled missile—seemed to take place almost overnight. At the same time improvements in communications were keeping pace. With the combination of improvements in transportation and communication even remote communities became closely allied and tied to all other major communities, both within a nation and between nations. These developments provided a basis for a much broader market for every industry. An industry that formerly was restricted to one town can now go out into a county or into a state with ease. Industry that had viewed its market as one state can now easily visualize national distribution. An industry that had felt itself limited by its national border looks with favorable eye toward international markets. But all these developments demand a much more advanced philosophy of management, broader planning, and greater reliance on each individual to support a greater and greater share of the accomplishment.

With the combination, then, of higher speeds and closer tolerances, larger losses than formerly are possible at any individual work place along the line. Because of the much greater impact of those losses and the greater complexity of operations, it becomes increasingly difficult for an executive to maintain control of his operations. The normal tendency is to use management methods carried over from the early industrial days. A company naturally gravitates toward a greater centralization of control. Individuals down the line are fitted into more closely circumscribed niches, where they are expected to follow the close direction of centralized procedures. This attitude seems economically justified by the industrial engineering thinking touched off by the work of Frederick Taylor.

Procedures are carefully worked out. Engineering drawings become more and more detailed. Less and less reliance is placed on the individual's judgment or initiative, although greater consequences can result from errors or difficulties down the line. Incongruously, less and less authority is delegated, even though the demands of every operation now suggest a broadening rather than a contracting of authority. Even the individual operator on a machine now has the power to control much greater losses or gains than was formerly true because of the increased capital investment at his command. Because of the complexity of an enterprise and the tightened timing requirements, each individual employee may affect an operation more seriously.

In order to control this sprawling, expensive, and complicated industrial machine, centralized accounting systems come into prominence. Budgets seem to be the natural answer. By reviewing a mass of figures a top manager feels he has control, forgetting that figures in and of themselves do not control men, their ambitions, their drives, their initiative, or the exercise of their judgment. Financial wizards tend to have the ascendancy.

Down below discontent arises. Management people at all levels do not develop as expected. Companies experience difficulty in finding leadership material to promote and politics creeps into the operation. Labor-management problems multiply. Demands for security clauses, seniority clauses, and many other concessions become highlighted.

To the top executive all these occurrences suggest a need for tighter and tighter control. So more procedures are developed; staff men spring up for every problem. More figures and more budgets are worked out; but at the same time less consideration is actually given to the personal needs of the man as he works in the industrial environment. Industry is accused of developing the "organization man." According to this accusation the epitome of a good manager at lower and middle levels becomes the agreeable, unprotesting individual who "fits in." The new thinker, the experimenter, or the critic is replaced by the man who wears well, is agreeable, and is a good committee member.

The feeling of dissatisfaction of the individual down the line becomes heightened, however, by the higher degree of social consciousness that develops in any civilization as it advances. Higher levels of education for more people develop more demands and a higher feeling of personal worth in a greater number of people. Broader voting rights brew more political pressure, so that governmental participation and interference in business is accentuated. With increased standards of living and higher educational opportunities, employees expect more recognition of their basic wants as individuals. These broader expectations cannot be met by any autocratic approach nor by the cog-in-the-machine theory underlying centralized operation. Democracy expects higher and higher production and with it an increasing recognition of the individual. It is probable that democracy can flourish only if both these expectations are met. The two must go ahead together. This is the major management challenge.

It is our belief that this challenge can best be met by

what we would call "results management." It is the aim of this type of management to integrate the work of the individual toward the over-all objectives of the institution with his own personal interests and desires. From this point of view the job of managing requires a deeper analysis of the objectives of the institution as they carry down the line. At the same time the basic objectives and interests of each individual must be examined and satisfied successfully. In other words, the individual must get his personal satisfactions at the same time that higher and higher output develops. This means that the prime job of management is to foster a work climate that encourages individuals to develop and broaden to their fullest capacities at the same time that they are shouldering their individual part of the responsibility for achieving the objectives of the enterprise.

Sound management is based on principle. The following chapters attempt to point up a series of principles that lead to more successful operation in any management situation if applied properly. We should point out, however, that management principles merely indicate influences. Other things being equal, a principle will tend to push in a certain direction. In a particular problem a number of principles may apply. The management decision that is made is almost always a compromise—a weighing of the relative importance of each principle in that particular case.

2

Delegation by Results

THE FUNCTION of management begins whenever the work to be accomplished is too much for one man. He must then get an assistant to whom he delegates some of the work he has to do. The basic way he delegates this work, or the requirement for accomplishment, will greatly influence the work of the man.

The supervisor wants to be sure that the man does not just work hard, but that he gets high output. He wants to avoid the problem of getting high-quality output but very little of it. He may be concerned about the fact that a man may tend to stretch out work, that there may be a tendency to soldier on the job. He would like to guard against the situation where a man may spend a great deal of time fussing, reviewing, and planning but accomplish little—perhaps a man goes through a great deal of motion but never finishes anything.

All sound delegation starts essentially the same way. A man (*A*, Figure 1) has certain results to accomplish. These are too much or too difficult for him to get done, so he asks another man (*B*) to accomplish part of them. What remains is still too much for him so he asks another man (*C*) to accomplish another part. Perhaps these accomplishments are too much for *B* and *C* so they, in turn, ask other men

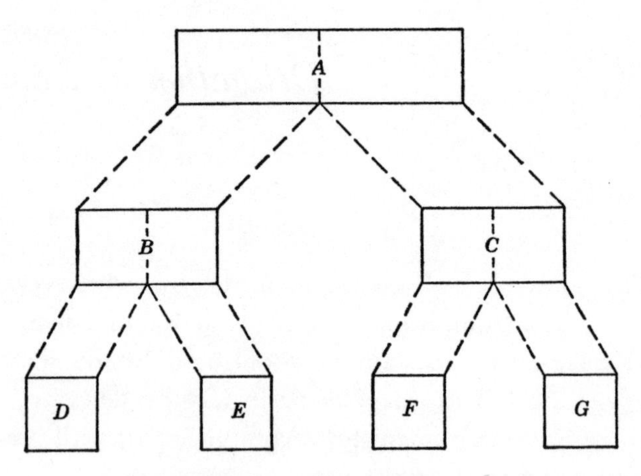

FIG. 1 Flow of delegation.

to accomplish parts of the results expected of them (*D, E, F,* and *G*). So delegation expands for any size of organization. The results expected of any one man should be part and parcel of those expected of the man above and finally of the results expected of the enterprise. The results expected of a subordinate can never be determined soundly until the results expected of his superior have been clarified. When this is done every man in the hierarchy is tied in soundly to his superior. It is to the superior's advantage to make his subordinates successful. He will then be successful himself.

We should emphasize that the key in delegation is to *delegate by the results that you expect of the man.* You can readily see that we are not talking about activities. The normal human inclination, however, is to delegate by activities or duties; to ask a man to do certain things; to make a long list of duties you want him to perform. For example, in many organization descriptions, organizing duties, planning duties, and coordinating duties are defined. Superficially this "duties" approach appears sound. To the man concerned it tends to be confusing because the real accomplishment expected of him becomes obscure. In addition, the emphasis that may be required on certain parts of his work becomes clouded, and all items take on a uniform importance. A great deal of interpretation may be needed to make the expected job accomplishments reasonably clear to the man. The emphasis on activities also tends to restrict authority. Until you have defined the results expected of a man you have not completed a delegation.

To elaborate further, you might say to a man, "Turn out 1,000 units per month with a maximum of 1 per cent waste." You would not say, "Keep the milling machines running on these castings to turn out this type of unit." Or you may say, "Secure $50,000 worth of sales this year from this territory, and in addition, make sure that we get 10 new dealers." You would not say, "Contact the dealers in this territory, set up displays, help train their sales people, and sell, sell, sell more products." Or you might say, "Develop a product which we can produce on the machines in our plant at a (specific) cost and which has sales appeal that would provide a payoff in profit within two years after it gets on the market." You would not say, "Investigate possible products for us, research them, develop various plans, run pilot studies, make analyses of alternative products, and study the design and cost pictures of these products." You will note that in each of these cases there is a distinct difference between specifying what the final outcome would be as against describing the activities or processes by which the man may arrive at the results. The latter approach so frequently leads to extra work, extra time, confusion, and often misunderstanding, culminating in high cost compared to actual accomplishments. In our estimation, this is the first, basic, and most important concept in sound management. What follows depends on this.

Every job in the enterprise is important; otherwise it should not be there. However, every position has more important and less important results. It is the job of the manager at any level to weigh the important versus the less important results (generally by money return or overall effect on the objectives of the enterprise). If there is a key item that could make or break the operation, the supervisor should stay very close to this. On the other hand, there may be a series of other operations which could go wrong, but only in a minor way at one time. These he could ordinarily delegate to a subordinate. He should carefully analyze every detail or duty with this in mind, recognizing, first, that there is a physical limit to the amount of work he can do effectively himself, and second, that other people usually have much greater abilities than we give them credit for. In general, the *less important results and details should be delegated,* and the *more im-*

portant results and broader decisions should be retained. This tends to get the best men on the most valuable work.

There is a normal tendency on the part of any man to retain work at which he may be especially adept or which he likes to do. A man who has just been promoted to a supervisory position is especially vulnerable to this tendency. It militates against sound delegation. For example, suppose the man is promoted from job *C* to job *B*. His natural inclination is to carry part of the activity with him (to *B*) instead of delegating it—usually the part he does very well or the part he likes to do. The responsibility for the results that have been delegated to his subordinate is thereby diluted. The subordinate generally feels relieved of accountability for the over-all result. Such a setup will lead to less accomplishment, particularly on the "sticky" parts of the work. In addition the supervisor may find that some of the work of his own job which could pay off to a much greater extent will tend to go by the board because he does not have time for it. The total accomplishment will then be less. When the man is promoted to *A*, this may be further complicated because he now carries some of the work of *B* and *C* along with him.

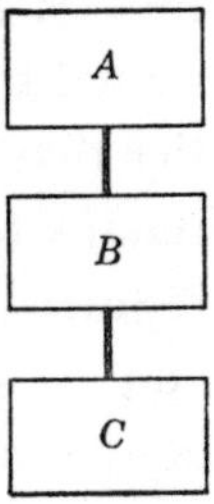

A

B

C

If the supervisor follows the philosophy of delegating only those things that he feels others can do well, he will also tend to retain less important work. In actual practice, if he were to weigh its importance against that of other items, the work would probably not stack up. It should be delegated.

Some executives suggest that a supervisor should delegate everything that others can do. We do not agree with this. Both the supervisor and his subordinates might be able to do some particular work. The key factor, however, is this: If the importance of that work is overriding, the supervisor himself must either do it or stay very close to it.

A normal occupational disease tends to afflict a supervisor at any level, that of succumbing to the belief that he himself is especially endowed with farseeing abilities not shared by his subordinates. One evidence of this is the belief that only he can plan ahead effectively. He therefore retains for himself the planning for any accomplishment required of the subordinate and expects the man to simply "do"—"yours but to do or die." The natural consequence of this attitude is that the man below does not feel accountable for the total accomplishment—he only controls part of the work (he doesn't do the planning). He may be continually caught short by "unexpected" items that come up. They were not planned for. He always has the alibi that he didn't know they were going to happen and he isn't expected to plan for them. As a consequence the man above is constantly swamped trying to anticipate and predict where the next crisis will occur. It is difficult at best to plan for every contingency when one is even one degree removed from a job.

In actual practice, the man on the job, when encouraged to do so, can often plan his own work better than can his superior, because he has more current facts at his immediate disposal. In general, therefore, this principle should apply: *Whenever a man has a responsibility for a result, he should also have the responsibility for planning ahead to prevent crises that may prevent the accomplishment of that result.* It is a common fallacy to assume that all planning should be done at the top. On the contrary, as much planning as possible should be encouraged within every job along with the responsibility for a result.

Many supervisors assume in their delegation that if a delegated result requires a decision beyond the authority of the subordinate, the man cannot be held accountable. Authority to recommend is not visualized as a form of authority. A kind of no man's land of action may emerge in many of these planning activities. The supervisor may then retain many activities that he should have delegated, or else many "unassigned" responsibilities may develop between the supervisor and the man, leading to slipshod operation.

A good way to reduce this difficulty is to force a broader planning concept into every job. Ordinarily, a man should have the responsibility to plan ahead for any accomplishment delegated to him. *In the event that a decision is necessary that the man is unable to make, he should also have a responsibility for making an analysis of the problem and presenting his recommendations to his superior*—the rule of completed function. It prevents the hiatus between the authority of the man and that of the boss—very often the source of misunderstandings, bottlenecks, and lack of accomplishment.

For example, a supervisor of a plant department may not have the authority to change an over-all scheduling activity. He should have both the responsibility and the authority, however, to study such a scheduling activity as it affects his operation and to recommend changes that would lead to a simplified and more efficient operation for him. In many cases he can develop a better approach to his problem. Without this responsibility he tends to have too easy an "out" in the event a problem occurs.

The same kind of problem could occur in any other activity. In sales work it is common to hear the comment, "Sales policy just won't permit me," as an excuse. If sales policy is excessively restrictive, the man should recommend a change that would permit greater sales effectiveness in his area. This would be true at any level—salesman, district manager, sales manager, or vice-president.

Just a comment in regard to the vice-president. Frequently function heads feel that the development of policy is the job of the top executive. The top executive, in turn, tends to feel that his function heads should develop policy. A gap in thinking occurs here. Ordinarily the same rules should apply to vice-presidents who are function heads as apply to men down the line. It is their obligation to develop needed policy and present it as their recommendation. Part of their responsibility should be the requirement to plan ahead on policy in their respective fields. Ordinarily they are the company experts in their fields and should be the best equipped to do this.

You can readily see that this approach to delegation leads to an over-all design of a lower position that would make it in a smaller way a replica of the job above. In other words, every job at every level tends to be a small duplicate of the job above rather than merely an "assistant" to the immediate superior. In such an environment men become broader-gauge. Their potential is much greater than was formerly realized. By this means, you lead to a greater fulfillment of the individual in that you can better capitalize on his personal initiative and ingenuity and give him scope. Men are more promotable. Experience in lower jobs makes men much more suitable to adequately fill vacancies in higher jobs. Lack of promotable men is less of a problem. At the same time the operation becomes smoother, more effective, with fewer "unexpected" problems. Each part is assigned to an individual.

In deciding what results he expects of a man, the supervisor is presumably figuring out the best way to achieve the greatest total accomplishment. Each result he assigns to a man is important and needed to get the total accomplishment. He should *expect the man to accomplish each of the results delegated to him.* And this should be emphasized to the man. If the man decides on his own that some results need not be accomplished, he is, in effect, deciding his own delegation. Frequently the initial trouble between a supervisor and a subordinate begins here. The man may decide to concentrate on one or two items instead of all of the items specified by the superior. Perhaps he likes part of the work better; or he may not be aware of the tie-in of his own with other work. Under these circumstances imbalanced situations will occur, creating bottlenecks, gaps, and slippages in almost any operation.

It is also important that all results should blend into the over-all intended direction of the enterprise. Short-range accomplishments must blend into the long-range objectives of the firm or new crises will constantly develop in an operation. Problems mushroom that had not been planned for. A special drive on some projects will lead to other problems in the future. Important areas that should have been developed never quite come through on time, so that more problems are experienced in the future. In sales, competition appears much more aggressive. All of these occurrences can be indications that the firm was focusing on short-range results without enough regard for long-range implications. *Specific results expected must be designed so that they encourage the man on the job to blend short-range into long-range.*

For example, if a salesman is pushed to get volume alone (as is true in many straight commission plans), he may not be building his territory soundly for the future. On the other hand, if he is required to get a certain number of new accounts or get a distribution of accounts from all parts of his territory, he may be automatically gearing his activities to build a strong over-all territory for the future. To assure that the firm is getting a foothold with the new products so that they are entrenched in the future he may be required to obtain a specific volume on certain new products. This same approach, of course, holds true for any level in the operation. The man is tied to the long-range goals of the firm because he gets personal recognition for his contribution to them.

The same problem can exist in a plant. A man may put all his effort into turning out as much production as possible at a particular time. This may have been encouraged because the firm had no sales problem and could sell everything it could produce. All the pressure on the man indicated that he would be best recognized for turning out a large volume of goods even though costs were high. As a consequence, he may overwork his machines and not maintain them properly. His quality may be relatively poor, and he may not be concerned about waste. He may also develop a very negative approach to method improvements. (Temporarily, or even permanently, they may interfere with volume of output.) The total effect of these conditions could lead to a complete negation of the value of current results because of the losses of the future.

Engineering may also suffer from this same problem. Engineers may design each machine independently to meet a current need, but no master plan is developed. Over a period of time a plant may become a hodgepodge of inflexible machinery ill adapted to gradual conversion to conveyorized operation. The engineer himself does not develop to be a broad-gauge man. He has not been forced to plan more broadly and fit his over-all function into that of the enterprise he is serving. Long-range implications must always be carefully considered in defining the results expected of any man.

3

The Basic Management Design—Management Objectives

INDIVIDUALS MAY easily get out of touch with the central purpose of the enterprise, a process encouraged by the natural inclination to specify the activities that are required of a man instead of the results. But even though there has been a general statement of the results that should normally be expected of a position, the definition process has not gone far enough unless specific objectives have been well set for all management people in the enterprise. Objectives should be set for personnel all the way down to each foreman and salesman and, in addition, to staff people such as accountants, industrial engineers, chemists, etc. It is only then that the individual becomes personally and positively involved in the success of the enterprise. He has his definite part to play.

What are objectives? Objectives are really a means for carrying delegation down to a specific period, probably one year. **Management objectives state the specific accomplishment expected of each individual in a specific period of time so that the work of the whole management group is soundly blended at a particular moment of time.** Each one has a known accomplishment to make leading to the over-all accomplishment expected of the enterprise in that period. To the extent that this is well done, each man knows exactly what is expected of him. To the extent that it is poorly done, delegation is weak, leading inevitably to weak operation, to weak accomplishment, and to a division of interest between the enterprise and the men, no matter what the level.

Because of the interweaving and necessary blending of the work of a number of people to get a final corporate accomplishment, it often seems difficult to set specific objectives for certain positions. It may seem especially difficult to define objectives that are measurable because of the record system in the firm. There is then a natural tendency to define activities rather than results with the rationalization that the activities, if properly carried out, will lead to the hoped-for result. This is very often wishful thinking. In almost every activity there is quite a broad range for interpretation of the direction it could take if end results have not been defined. Under these conditions the individual on the job will often make interpretations counter to those made by his superior. The accomplishment is then less than was expected and perhaps in a different direction. In addition, difference in interpretation may give the man the impression that the rules have been changed on him during the period. He will lose some of his enthusiasm.

To the extent that you can *state the objectives in terms of final measurable results,* such as dollars, percentages, amounts, etc., you tend to get better understanding and better direction. The man is encouraged to accept the philosophy that he **does** have to contribute to the actual accomplishment of the enterprise in this particular period. Without measurable objectives, this point is very frequently missed at various levels in the operation. The man may become divorced from the central drive of the enterprise.

One of the stumbling blocks in the way of setting measurable objectives is that the record system does not appear to be good enough to measure progress toward objectives with accuracy. We should point out that extreme accuracy is not critical. In many cases, *crude measurements are serviceable* to start out with. They are often adequate permanently. One of the common errors in going into an objective program is the assumption that there must be completely measurable results and that the measurement must be perfectly accurate. In many cases, this is almost an impossibility. Even if the measurement is somewhat inaccurate, men are better stimulated with measurable objectives than without them. They better understand the direction of the enterprise and their own responsibility in it.

UNDERLYING PRINCIPLES OF MANAGEMENT OBJECTIVES

In an effort to cover all parts of a position, managers will frequently try to define everything that they wish a position to accomplish. Because job descriptions often attempt to describe all the duties of a job, each duty is used as a basis for an objective. This inevitably leads to objectives on many subparts of a job, frequently minor subparts. Very often these objectives are simply phases of projects and cannot be measured in terms of final result. The manager feels quite satisfied, however, with having completely outlined "all the parts" of the position. He may wind up with anywhere from 10 to 30 specific items. He has "completely" described the requirements of the job (see Figure 2).

The difficulty is that the individual on the job may actually be steered away from final results by this catalogue list. He often fails to see the final accomplishment to which some of the minor results should be contributing. In addition, he is not given as much leeway to pick and choose and blend these minor items to get the best overall total accomplishment. He is restricted in the judgment he may exercise. In a sense, the specific items tend to reduce his authority and leeway to take action. There is also a tendency for a man to feel secure in the accomplishment of, say, 90 per cent of these minor items even though 10 per cent were not accomplished. The 10 per cent not accomplished may be more difficult and more important, however, so that the net accomplishment is considerably less than 90 per cent. The catalogue list approach generally does not give proper emphasis to the most important items. It can therefore easily lead a man away from maximum valuable accomplishment.

Too many objectives tend to take the drive out of an objective program. As a working rule, *no position should have more than two to five objectives.* If there are more, they should ordinarily be combined in some way. A program with too many objectives tends to highlight the minor ones to the detriment of the major ones. Any objective

---

To approve purchase requisitions in his office
To plan budget requests for his operations
To develop plant production policies
To supervise production scheduling methods; to make sure that Sales is notified of promise dates
To make sure that new construction is adequately supervised
To recommend appropriate incentive systems for his production employees
To supervise activities of repair, quality, material handling, plant engineering and get maximum efficiency from them
To determine methods of handling obsolete equipment
To aid in development of by-product uses
To establish a policy for technical services in his departments
To determine standards for processes and equipment
To provide staff services for planning new construction
To get all his employees to be on the alert for patentable items
To recommend equipment needed
To determine industrial engineering policy
To supervise production office
To maintain control over plant inventories

FIG. 2 Typical "duties" type of description, often used instead of "results" statements.

that is less than 10 or 15 per cent of the job should probably be combined with another one.

Even though a small number of objectives has been set, the man on the job may weigh them differently from the way his superior does. For example, he may feel that all objectives are of equal value. This is rarely the case. Or he may feel that one objective overrides all others. A typical example of this is in purchasing, where price of goods purchased is often held to be **the** important item. (Such an emphasis usually comes from past experience of commendation or reprimand.) In many cases, this may not be true. Timing of deliveries, quality of materials, packaging, and inventory investment may be as important, and in some cases even more important.

When you *assign a percentage value to objectives,* they become much more effective. For example, if there are three objectives, the executive should be able to say that one objective is 40 per cent, another 40 per cent, and the third 20 per cent of the job. He will encourage a better-balanced effort from the man on the job. The delegating executive will be forced to do a much more realistic job of planning the results that he has to get. He will frequently find that objectives he believed to be important are so small in value compared with others that they should not be given special emphasis. They should, perhaps, be combined with other objectives. To the man on the job it becomes clear that he cannot get recognition for a job well done unless good accomplishment can be shown on each objective. The percentage weight of each one is too large to ignore.

With the growth of accounting records, particularly since

the advent of high-speed data-processing equipment, there is a greater and greater tendency to centralize record control. These records usually tend to highlight costs and may lead to what can be an undermining characteristic in any operation, that of overemphasizing costs to the detriment of the creative goals of a position. Ordinarily, any position is set up to accomplish something, not necessarily to control costs. This point is frequently lost sight of when objectives are set directly from a P & L statement or a cost statement, as they are likely to be. (It is true, of course, that the accomplishment should be made as efficiently as possible so that costs can be held under control.)

It is usually advantageous for an executive to *first set the creative goals of a position.* What is the accomplishment to be made that will forward the enterprise? Is it to get sales, produce a product, make loans, or give a service? Secondarily, *then, cost objectives* should enter the picture. Ask yourself first in regard to the job, "What is the reason for its existence? What is it supposed to contribute?" Then, and only then, should you ask yourself, "What is the estimated cost that we can permit in order to get this result?" In other words, you should look at cost in light of accomplishment. One of the most expensive violations of this principle can occur in sales. While sales cost is important, sales accomplishment, whether represented in terms of more volume, more outlets, better price, or better tie-in to plant operation, is probably the first essential. Then, secondarily, the cost of realizing the creative goals must be kept within reason. Salesmen who are badgered by cost considerations may do less creative selling.

The same philosophy can apply to other positions, however. For example, in plants or offices emphasis on costs (very frequently through budgets) may easily develop a philosophy that one should not take chances and spend money on new methods. New methods may be a gamble and throw off the budget. The discouragement of improvement is one of the most enervating effects of overemphasis on cost. Management people at all levels may be subtly discouraged from creatively experimenting with new or improved methods.

Some executives feel that it is good practice to set objectives that are far out in "the wild blue yonder." In other words, they feel that it is sound to set objectives that are almost impossible to attain. "Give them something to shoot for." This philosophy is ordinarily based on an unrealistic approach to human beings and their motivation. *Objectives should be reasonable.* It takes a great deal of fortitude and drive for a man to consistently react well to an objective set beyond his reach. In most cases such an objective will take the heart out of a good man rather than be a stimulus to him to work harder. People are usually more stimulated by success than they are by failure. In addition, if goals are too stiff, a man may begin to accept nonaccomplishment as normal and lose his sense of personal accountability—the real driving force that spurs men on in any operation. The bad effect of stiff goals was demonstrated by an executive who was perfectly willing to specify a 10-million-dollar sales volume goal for a branch where 6 million had been the highest ever achieved in the past. There was comparatively little drive toward high goals in that firm. Instead, there was a constant flow of alibis, cover-ups, and reasons for lack of accomplishment.

Many executives feel that any one responsibility can be delegated to only one individual. This feeling appears to grow stronger when specific objectives are discussed. Such an attitude, however, can lead to an unrealistic approach to management operation. It is not only perfectly proper, but almost essential, that *objectives should be set for a man in any area where he has a strong influence on the result even though he does not have full control.* This will mean that the same objective may be set for more than one person. In actual practice it is a rare objective that does not require the work of more than one person for accomplishment. Setting the same objective for two people forces sound cooperation between men—in time schedules, quality of work, etc. It makes the accomplishment of the objective of value to both men. Cooperation becomes increasingly a part of normal operation. It is advantageous to each of the two men to cooperate in order to achieve the result. Lack of accomplishment will react to the disadvantage of each. The accomplishment of the objective will redound to their mutual advantage, generally a more effective spur to effort than exhortations to "cooperate" or to be good company men. Contrary to the belief of many executives, one of the major values of a sound objective program is that it makes cooperation advantageous to the individuals in the firm. It encourages rather than discourages cooperation.

In our competitive economy, firms must constantly improve or they are left by the wayside. Improvement must become a way of life for every person in the enterprise. Unfortunately, a counterphilosophy often develops that improvement is a responsibility of a certain small number of individuals, very frequently staff men or higher management men. As a consequence, management people down the line do not embrace improvement as part of their individual responsibility. Improvement will not come automatically. It must be built in as part of the basic organization setup. (It is extraordinary how much creative ability often lies dormant in individuals. Management objectives provide one of the soundest ways we know of for tapping this ability.) *Objectives should require some improvement in operation from each man every period.* They provide a basis for recognition of improvement for each man.

Without objectives it is common for management to demand improvement in some areas but not in others. As a consequence many management people feel that last year's methods are good enough. Such a feeling should be discouraged. Objectives should force some improvement in every position every year. After all, good performance last year is easier for the man to attain this year. He ordinarily has last year's gains to help him. A word of caution! Improvement means improvement in method, not necessarily in results. For example, a 10 per cent decline in sales volume may reflect substantial improvement if the industry has declined 20 per cent.

This improvement philosophy appears to be at odds with the normal industrial engineering approach in time-study incentive plans, where there is usually a guarantee that the standard will hold indefinitely unless the procedure changes. This approach is not sound when applied to management people. In effect, the standard changes every year. A little better job is required. However, there is more consistency with the industrial engineering approach than at first appears. The achievement of last year will probably be easier this year. An average job done by a man applying himself reasonably well should be better this year than it was the year before. He has the new ideas that were developed the year before to work on. His job is easier.

If you do not write into the job requirement a specific accountability for some improvement every year, you have taken the first step toward a relaxation of individual drive. The very setup will eventually develop a lagging, desultory, and nonaggressive team. As the firm grows it will frequently find itself faced with key openings and no one to fill them. Its men will not grow to realize the full potential of their own abilities. Management has not been developed to man new positions and to meet new challenges. A firm is well on the way to this stagnation if it allows a new idea to be killed with the comment, "We're doing all right. We are better off than the industry"; or, "We don't want to stir up any trouble now. Things are going all right."

Closely allied to the question of improvement is the question of changing objectives. As we stated earlier, objectives reflect the requirement for accomplishment for a particular year. It is part of any changing enterprise that requirements, and therefore *objectives, should change from year to year.* What was most important one year may be of lesser importance the following year. Operating conditions change, companies change, and outside conditions change. One of the great advantages of objectives is that they force flexibility. They should be carefully reviewed at the beginning of every period so that they will reflect those changes in conditions that must be met. The firm will be more virile and up to date. It is unrealistic to assume that objectives or requirements will not change from period to period in any dynamic company. In fact, one of the reasons for the gradual relaxation of employees in many firms is the almost unconscious acceptance of the fact that, once set up, requirements should hold for years to come. This change in philosophy must, of course, be sold to all management people as being part of normal operation.

Generally, *objectives are most effective if they are set in advance of the period they are to cover.* There is a tendency on the part of a number of executives to want to have all the facts available before they set any objectives. They suffer from the fear that an objective may be set that is either too tight or too loose, generally the latter. As a consequence, when they set objectives they frequently set them later in the period. You can readily see the effect of this on the employee. He probably believes that the executive has made sure of his performance and then set the objective so that he will get a certain amount of recognition but no more. In addition, the man does not have the full period in which to work toward the accomplishment of the objectives. Much of the stimulating effect of objectives may be lost. A flagrant example of this error was made by a large mill supply manufacturer where sales managers' objectives—and incidentally, bonus plans—were issued on the first of September for the current calendar year. You can well imagine the effect on the employees concerned.

Objectives should ordinarily be in writing, with a copy for the man and a copy for his boss. We should point out, however, that the fact that they are in writing is not significant except as a matter of reference. Objectives should always be discussed face to face between the supervisor and the man until they are mutually understood and accepted. The copy in writing is merely a reflection of an understanding that has been arrived at personally. In every case, of course, it is *the supervisor* who *should make sure that his men have a clear understanding of these objectives.* The subordinate is always at a disadvantage if he must take the initiative in this.

4

The Dynamics of Management Objectives

If management is to obtain the best possible blending of the interests of the individual with those of the corporation, extreme care must be exercised in getting objectives down to the man concerned. Both the process of objective setting and the application of objectives to the individual must be realistic as they affect human beings, their individual motivations, their interests, their normal reactions. Since the purpose is to stimulate the man, these human factors are all-important in obtaining the greatest value from objectives. Many companies err in this area because they accept too easilv the authoritarian approach which assumes simply that delegations come from above and are referred downward. Organizationally speaking, this is sound. Delegations are determined by the superior. If you want to make that delegation effective and most earnestly embraced by the subordinate, however, a whole series of principles of motivation must be observed.

OBJECTIVES SHOULD BE A STIMULUS

First of all, *any objective must be set in light of all known existing conditions.* The determination of these conditions includes an evaluation of past history, of competition, of the impact of other people in the enterprise on the man, and of any obstacles that may prevent his accomplishing results. When the conditions change, the objectives should change.

The superior should *set both basic and outstanding performance objectives for each result.* He would do this by first asking himself, "In light of all the conditions as I know them, what would be reasonable job performance on this particular result?" Reasonable job performance usually means the answer to this question: If you had an experienced man who understood the job well, what might be considered reasonably good performance for him (not outstanding and not poor)? Ordinarily, anyone who would be kept on the payroll over a period of time should be expected to attain a performance of this level. Determine specifically what the objective should be and state this as the basic performance objective (see Figure 3).

A superior should then ask himself further, "In the light of all these same conditions, what would I consider to be an **outstanding** job?" In other words, define very good performance that could be achieved by a good man with high effort. A word of caution in this regard: "Outstanding" in this case would mean that the individual, by extra application or insight, would probably be able to reach this level. It should not be something almost unattainable out yonder. It should be attainable by a man doing a very good job under the conditions as envisioned for the coming year. This should then be set as the outstanding objective. You have determined the basic accomplishment expected of a man if he works well and in the right direction,

Result area	Basic performance objective	Outstanding performance objective
1. Sales volume	$100,000	$140,000
2. Sales outlets	10 new outlets	16 new outlets
3. Development of a product	$150,000 profit in first 2 years after paying all development costs	$300,000 profit in first 2 years after paying all development costs
4. Cases completed	8 per day	11 per day
5. Meet schedules	90% of the time.	98% of the time

FIG. 3 Examples of objectives.

and, in addition, you have set what he should shoot for in order to be recognized as outstanding. Do the same thing for each of the major results expected of him in the period.

Many executives make the mistake of setting only one figure for an objective. Ordinarily they have only a loose idea as to whether it would represent normal or outstanding accomplishment. Should the man work hard and apparently accomplish the objective with ease (which happens frequently when men are set up against specific objectives), a subtle change develops in the mind of the superior. He tends to minimize the accomplishment of the subordinate. He feels that his objective was too loose in the first place. Much of the stimulus is taken away from the employee in that he feels that he has been tricked. Should the man, however, have some difficulty in accomplishing the objective, there is a tendency to view the objective then as something to be striven for but not necessarily attained. Both the man and the superior begin to look at the objective as something that the man is not accountable for. One of the common errors managers make in setting objectives is that they do not set both the basic and the outstanding accomplishment expected for each item.

Another common error made by managers is to assume that objectives apply to the job and not to the individual. This error can spoil a good man as he enters a job. It is worthwhile having a man work against objectives even when he is comparatively new on the job (after his initial training period). However, *objectives for a new man should be set in light of his experience.* In other words, one of the conditions affecting the setting of objectives is the lack of experience of the man (on this particular job). On reflection it is perfectly logical that both the basic and the outstanding accomplishment expected of a beginner on a job would not be as high as that of an experienced man. Setting lower objectives for new men has important implications later on when determining their authority. Since authority should be set in light of objectives or accomplishment expected, the superior will then automatically consider authority for the beginner realistically.

Should you set the same objective for a beginner as you would for an experienced man, you may set the stage for failure. The man may do his best to achieve his objectives. In doing this he may step out of line and make errors which will cast a reflection on him for years to come, a situation with serious implications for the future for a young manager, say, who is in one of his early management positions. On the other hand, he may simply give up, knowing full well that it will be almost impossible for him to achieve these objectives. His superior permits this, since the man is new. The man then develops an unsatisfactory lack of accountability for objectives. He will be weakened for the future.

If a firm is large and has both staff and line people, it is helpful to *set the line objectives first.* Since these focus on the central service the enterprise is to provide, the basic company accomplishment is highlighted. After this, staff objectives should be set so that they are harmonious with those objectives set for the line. (Staff provides service functions aimed at helping the line do its job better—see Chapter 15, page 185.)

One of the most difficult phases of setting objectives is that of making each objective harmonious with others. A man who is working toward an objective may become impervious to the needs of other people in the firm. Objectives may accentuate "lone wolf" inclinations. Therefore, after all objectives have been set in a preliminary way, it is well to write them down and *cross-check to see that all objectives blend with each other.* The individual objectives for each man must be studied in their implication to see whether or not they will interfere with the objectives of other men. If so, adjustment should be made so that it is to the advantage of one man to help another.

Objectives should also be cross-checked upward so that the objectives of any man tie into those of his superior and eventually into the objectives of the enterprise. If this is done carefully, each echelon is allied with the echelons above. All are encouraged to work together toward an over-all company objective. They are all on the same team and heading in the same direction. If a subordinate fails, the superior shares his failure. This cross check puts a great deal more strength behind any objective program. It sets up a basis for realistic accountability, tying all levels of the organization together effectively. Better communications are encouraged. They become more realistic, as they are now part of a natural management flow. They are essential for the smooth working toward objectives.

A strong drive toward one particular result may lead to imbalance in the company. Very often there is an optimum level beyond which an achievement may actually be harmful to some other objective of the firm. In a plant, quality control carried too far may have detrimental effects on waste and on cost of production. In a procurement department, getting the material in on time may raise costs by not allowing time to get several bids. Each objective should be carefully scrutinized to determine the optimum point beyond which the objective might be detrimental to the achievement of other objectives. Setting the outstanding objective and giving no credit for accomplishment beyond it will minimize excessive pressure on any one result. To this extent such a limitation encourages further concentration on other objectives.

Another way to prevent imbalance is to set a counter-objective. For example, a purchasing agent may be held accountable for both a level of inventory and for down time due to lack of materials. Going too far on one generally affects the other. A built-in type of self-discipline is provided whereby the man can regulate himself. The need for constant checks by supervision is minimized, and the wise exercise of judgment by the purchasing agent is encouraged.

One loan company increased its volume of business (and profits) substantially by arbitrarily setting up a higher loss ratio. They were then able to accept much more of the business that came to the counter. They could do this profitably at a comparatively low cost, and as a consequence their net profits were more than enough to overcome the added credit losses they incurred.

People trained in precise figure work, such as engineering and accounting people, are inclined to feel that once objectives are set the job is done. Nothing could be farther from the truth. The prime value of an objective is in the stimulation of a man. The emotional impact on the man must, therefore, be carefully considered when objectives are installed. If objectives are to stimulate *the man,* he *must feel that the objectives are fair.* It is not enough that they are actually fair; what is important is that the man **feels** that they are fair. What makes him feel that they are fair? A man is usually much more sold on objectives if he participates in setting them. He understands them better and is better sold on their fairness. Resentment, opposition, and alibis generally develop if objectives are set above and simply handed down for compliance.

There is a difficulty, however. Essentially, objective setting is the job of the superior—it is the final expression of his delegation. How can you get the subordinate to set objectives and still avoid the violation of this superior-subordinate relationship? Ordinarily the following procedure works quite well: The superior should first discuss the general conditions under which the man will be working and in a broad way point out to the man the over-all expectation in company objectives. In a way he is pointing out the general track on which the total operation is running. It is also helpful for the superior to point out some of the places in the man's job where he thinks objectives might be especially worthwhile that year. He should then *ask the man* to take this information, carefully review his own sphere of action, and come back later *to suggest what he considers to be sound objectives* for himself. Ask him how he will shoulder his share of the total responsibility. Most men do not wish to be considered laggards. The man will often suggest much more difficult objectives for himself than his superior might otherwise have set. And note this! He will generally be more sold on their fairness than if someone else had forced him to accept these objectives.

An important additional benefit results from this method of setting objectives. Since a man has to go back and think through the objectives, he will think much more broadly than he would otherwise and plan ahead. He is usually careful to analyze his whole operation so that when he comes back with objectives he is fairly certain that he will be able to accomplish them. Before proposing objectives he will probably lay out a plan for reaching them. He becomes a broader man by the process, one who is able to plan ahead and think through problems without imposing them on his superior. Such a procedure places the planning function solidly on the subordinate's shoulders.

What if the man returns with objectives that are much higher than those his superior had been considering? There is a temptation for the superior to accept these higher objectives since the man himself set them. In most cases this would be a grave mistake. If the superior is still convinced that these objectives are higher than they should be, he should reduce them. This would be true either for basic or for outstanding performance or for both. A good way to do this is to tell the man, "I appreciate your interest in setting such difficult objectives, but I would be well satisfied if the following (lower) objectives were met. If you meet them, I'll still consider that you have done the job."

The impetus and drive that this approach gives to the man, and the confidence in the fairness of the superior, provide a strong stimulus. His general reaction is, "I can easily meet that." (Note the comment made earlier, that men are more stimulated by success than they are by failure.) Do not set tougher objectives for a man simply because he proposes them. If the subordinate shows in the discussion that the superior's first idea of sound objectives was really too loose, then it is perfectly all right to accept a higher objective. Since this is an easy rationalization for the superior, however, he should try to be very critical of this step before he takes it.

It is also helpful to ask the man to set percentage values for each of his objectives. The superior may then compare these with the percentages that he would have assigned and have a good basis for a discussion of the relative value of the different objectives. Both on the objectives and on the percentage values, however, the final decision still has to be made by the superior. Many managers find this participative procedure difficult to accept; they feel they are giving away some of their prerogative. Nothing is given away, because the man is still finally accountable for the accomplishment which has been agreed to by the superior. If the man should return with objectives that are too low, these would not be accepted. They would be used as a basis for a discussion with the man to build him up to accepting higher objectives.

It is very important that *the superior should adopt a positive attitude toward objective setting.* In other words, once objectives have been set, it should be tacitly assumed that they will be met. Otherwise a subordinate may develop a negative approach. He just can't meet them! This points up all the more the importance of setting reasonable objectives that can be met. Setting objectives that you assume will not be met or that would be extremely difficult to meet may very well take much of the steam out of the program. There is then a tendency for the man to "carp" too much and for the superior to be too quick to relieve a man of accountability because of some unusual condition. A part of the conditions under which objectives have been set should be the "normal" unpredictable occurrences that affect the job. It is assumed that the man will meet his objectives in spite of these conditions.

Many executives ask whether or not they should adjust objectives in the middle of the year should conditions change. Ordinarily the answer is no! Adjustments tend to weaken an objective program. However, there are some circumstances that may require an adjustment. These get right back to fairness to the individual. It is assumed that the normal give-and-take of a job is covered earlier in establishing the conditions. Objectives may be revised, however, if there is a radical change in the conditions assumed when setting the objectives. A mid-period review may be advisable to consider whether the conditions are actually as anticipated.

For example, one of these conditions might be the fact that a plant from which all products were to be sold in a given territory was burned down. It is quite obvious that no salesman could possibly sell high volume if he has few products to sell. His objectives may therefore be adjusted in light of the potential now available to him. The fact that competition was a little tougher than anticipated or that the economy went up or down 5 or 10 per cent should not change the objectives. Ordinarily, within these limits, objectives should hold for the year. The man is expected to carry the load for the company. Perhaps a 20 per cent drop in the potential may justify a change. If at the end of the year objectives prove to be wrong one way or the other, they may be adjusted or changed for the coming year. Any errors would be corrected then, because objectives would be reviewed for change anyway at the beginning of the year.

In some cases it may be perfectly sound to set sliding objectives in the beginning of the year and tie them to possible changes in key conditions. In a mail-order house a supervisor may have cost objectives tied to the number of orders sent in each week. If it is up, his cost objective is higher. If it is down, his cost objective is lower.

How should accomplishment on one objective be looked

at versus accomplishment on another? Very frequently an employee on a job may feel that one objective is much more difficult or much more valuable and put a great deal of time into it. As a consequence, he may achieve accomplishments far beyond the outstanding objective for that particular item. However, he may not even reach the basic performance on one of the other objectives. The objective that he focused on may actually prove to be worth more money in that particular period. Should the supervisor balance off the very superior accomplishment on one objective against the below-normal accomplishment on another? Let us examine what would happen if this were done. If he permitted this, he would, in effect, be allowing the man to determine his own delegation without the consent of the superior. In subsequent years the man would also pick and choose among the objectives irrespective of the percentage weights that had been agreed to for each. Severe imbalance in the operation could result.

Failure to accomplish a given objective may also seriously impinge on the work of other people in the operation so that serious losses may be incurred and bottlenecks develop. For example, concentration on one type of product in a plant department in order to get long runs may cause too many back orders. On the other hand, unbalanced sales volume may easily cause shutdowns of entire lines in a plant. The man concerned may not feel accountable for these losses. In order to maintain balance *the superior should require at least basic accomplishment on all objectives in each period.* If he does not, he will lose control of the operation. Unusual accomplishment on one objective should almost never be accepted as excusing of lack of accomplishment on other objectives. Otherwise the superior will not be able to depend on the man for balanced accomplishment in the future. Lack of balance is one of the most costly errors in most operations.

GETTING THE NEW OBJECTIVE PROGRAM INTO OPERATION

Frequently, the first reaction of managers considering a management-objective program is that they do not have enough figures or data on which to set objectives. It seems impossible to determine accurately what objectives or measurements should be used. Fortunately it is not necessary to require perfection in your objective program at the outset. *Crude objectives or measurements* that are not completely accurate *are usable in getting the program started.* Experience will later prove where they are in error. You can make adjustments in the next period. They will still operate as a better stimulus than not having them.

At the start records may not seem particularly well adapted to the objective program. Parts of a job may be hard to measure. There is therefore a tendency to retreat from objectives because the whole position cannot be covered. It does not have to be. In the beginning, concentrate on one or two of the major results such as cost reduction, sales increase, waste reduction, better schedule performance, etc., if this is all that you can do in light of the records available. You will still get the man to concentrate on an item that is important and will get him accustomed to operating under a mode of operation based on objectives.

Initially it is a good idea to select those items for which measurements are readily available even though they are somewhat crude. It is not essential that every facet of the job be covered in the first year. A perfectly workable plan might set objectives for only part of the job in the first year. Men develop a better understanding of objectives and will usually get improvement without forcing any major long-range imbalance. In subsequent periods all major parts of the job should be covered as soon as possible, however, or you will probably push toward an imbalanced operation.

When executives first approach an objective program, they often become very enthusiastic about it and try to accomplish the ultimate in the first year. There is something about the analysis that precedes objective setting that opens up one's eyes to possible improvements. A new millennium of perfection seems quickly within reach. It is not that easy! *Do not demand the ultimate the first year.*

If a 15 per cent improvement in the operation is possible, a manager often feels that this should be the objective for the first year. Nothing could be farther from the truth. You are much better off encouraging a 4 per cent improvement (something you may never have obtained before) in the first period. Some managers may react against such a suggestion, feeling that 4 per cent is not as much as he ought to demand since 15 per cent is possible (but the 15 per cent will probably not appear fair to his subordinates). In the following year he may get 5 per cent more, and perhaps 6 per cent in the third year. Eventually he would probably be up beyond 15 per cent. But note this! His men will get in the habit of meeting objectives. This is essential! They will be encouraged to use their own initiative to plan ahead, and will be spurred on by success, a much more effective stimulus in any case than failure. Men will develop much more rapidly and the firm will accomplish more in the long run.

5

Develop the Freedom to Act

In order to function well, any society must develop rules or mores, a recognized code of action that it imposes on its members. This is the adhesive that effectively binds the group together. The imposition may be through social pressure, or it may be through actual laws. The net effect, however, is that the individual leads to some extent a "permissive" existence. The particular community or religious groups within which a person matures tend to develop additional restrictions to the freedom of his action. A man learns by past experience, by criticism or praise, what is acceptable. This carries through all his existence and tends to formulate his approach to any new situation.

In a particular company this core code is expanded (and sometimes changed) by the experience a man has. The sum total of all a man's past work experiences suggests to him what is or what is not acceptable procedure. If at some time in the past he ventured out on some uncharted action and was sharply criticized for it, this indicates to him that similar types of action will be looked at similarly in spite of all the comments to the contrary. In the extreme case, he may develop a fear of taking any action, particularly when his past experiences suggest that he has been judged by no basic code but rather by a capricious series of unexpected criticisms. He then hesitates to make decisions, particularly on anything new. He is inclined toward voluminous reporting of all the conditions underlying a problem so that someone else may make a decision. He may develop special skill in alibis or cover-ups. These conditions may exist because of the failure of his superior to recognize the personal implication of authority, namely, that it means the freedom to act.

Each decision is in a sense a gamble. All possible adverse conditions can never be completely anticipated. In establishing the right to make decisions a manager must recognize that errors should occur as part of a normal operation if a man is making decisions. If authority is to open up the gates to the flood of ability stored in each individual, it must be approached from this point of view.

A common mistake is to look at authority simply from the management point of view and to consider it as the "right to command." This theory suggests that a man has authority whenever his superior gives it to him. In the superior's view he is giving "full authority." Authority becomes impersonal and almost entirely a downward autocratic process. The basic implication is that if you state something, it is automatically in effect. Such an approach entirely ignores the fact that authority is developed over a period of time by actual practice and experience. Authority is meaningless until the man on the job **feels** that he has it —that he has the right to make decisions.

A man must feel free to make a decision—especially in new situations, because these are generally where the problem occurs most forcefully. He does not really feel that he has authority if he has to get approval from his superior or review a decision with him ahead of time. He does not usually feel that he has authority to make decisions, no matter what is said, if he has to justify every change in the budget in writing or if all purchase orders require double signatures.

Authority takes on added importance in our technological economy when you get into the creative aspects of any institution. In the nature of the work, the man is probing in areas that are uncharted. It is difficult to make a decision without a high possibility of error. If the man is expected to take bold action, his past history must suggest to him that he must be somewhat daring and experimental, even though at times some substantial losses result. Industry must encourage this daring.

THE RULE OF ERRORS

How do you get a man to feel that he can make decisions? Usually by helping him lose his fear of making errors. How can you alleviate the fear of making an error? Generally, by applying what we call the Rule of Errors: *If a man has a responsibility for a result, he should be permitted to make the normal errors expected in making the normal decisions necessary to achieve that result.* He should be accountable at the end of the period for the total result and the total cost of getting the result, including the cost of the errors he incurred.

How do you define this for an actual job? First, the supervisor (and I emphasize only the supervisor) decides specifically what objectives he expects the man to accomplish in a given period. He must make sure the man understands and accepts them. Second, the supervisor should ask himself these questions: (1) "Considering all the conditions as we see them, what are the normal decisions that I or any one else would probably have to make in order to reach each objective?" (2) "If I, or any one else, made those decisions, what would be the risk of error?—What are the typical errors I would normally expect to make?" Third, he should then tell the man that he has the right to make these errors. He will not be reprimanded or criticized for them individually. They are assumed to be part of normal operation, **even for an outstanding man.** (If he makes greater errors than these, or if he makes more than the normal number, his decisions would be reviewed by the supervisor.) In effect this leeway gives the man more latitude in determining his mode of operation. He may experiment to some extent with different approaches. Fourth, at the end of the period the man should be called to account by the supervisor for his total accomplishment on each objective, balancing off total cost (including that of any errors made) against his total accomplishment. Fifth, if his net accomplishment is in line with the expected objective, no criticism should be given for the specific errors made.

Authority should be defined for each of the objectives expected of a man in a period. You can readily see that organization definition as we visualize it implies a review of authority at the beginning of every period in the light of the objectives that are specified for that period. In general, a broad cataloguing of over-all authority to hold for several years is impractical and meaningless to the man in a dynamic enterprise. A prime weakness in viewing authority has been the failure to relate it specifically to the objectives expected to be achieved within a particular period of time.

New jobs present a special problem when you consider the right to make errors. It often takes a long time to develop skill in an employee who is on a new job. He does not readily accept new functions. It is often difficult to determine authority limits on a new job. One reason for this is that you do not yet know the impact of an error. Broad statements in job descriptions are of little value in these cases. In practice, new jobs have to be set up with authority limits that are actually guesses. They should usually be on the liberal side. These limits should be reviewed within as short a time as possible so that sound authority to make decisions can be delegated. The failure to do this is sometimes the reason for the inordinate length of time necessary to get new tasks, functions, or jobs up to a sound, smooth, efficient operating level. The employee is not sure where he stands. He is afraid to take the bigger gambles that are necessary in these untried areas of his work.

If the definition of permissible error is not arrived at quickly in new positions, there is a tendency for the person on the job to do one of two things. He may become accustomed to doing very sloppy work, assuming an excessive numbers of errors as part of normal operation. Or, because of the pressure and discussion every time an error is made, he assumes that he should not make any errors or should always ask somebody else for advice before he does anything. Either situation leads toward poor operation and toward a poor development of the person on the job. It is therefore advantageous to work in new functions gradually and constantly observe the job setup for the changes in authority that are necessary in order to arrive at normal operating procedure.

The "errors" approach to authority gets away from criticism for minor errors. In fact, it forces a superior to put minor errors in their proper perspective. It is fairly obvious, of course, to any operating executive that this takes mental discipline on the part of the superior. It is extremely difficult to let someone make errors without making pointed comments.

It is difficult at best for a superior to know whether or not he is actually carrying through on the Rule of Errors so that his subordinates "feel" that they have authority. One rule-of-thumb test is this: If a subordinate will willingly come up to the superior and confess an error without alibiing or giving all the reasons why it occurred, the chances are that the superior is applying the Rule of Errors reasonably well. If subordinates either cover up or, when an error is discussed, are quick to present all sorts of alibis or reasons why it occurred, the chances are that they do not really feel that they have authority.

In a mistaken belief that they fully recognize the need

to delegate adequate authority, some executives frequently comment to their subordinates, "You can make an error once, but don't make it twice." The assumption is that they are giving the man perfect freedom to make errors but they are putting a hedge around it so that he will not repeat the same error. In effect, they are retracting authority. Think for a minute what would happen if a subordinate made an error once and then a similar problem occurred. There is a natural tendency for him to be hesitant about making a decision for fear that an error might occur that will appear to be similar to the error that was made before. In addition, some people hesitate unduly about making the first error for fear that they then will not have another chance. The executive's statement, in effect, retains authority instead of giving it. A true concept of authority puts little weight on the fact that the error may have occurred once before.

One of the reasons why managers hesitate to give authority and tend to be restrictive in regard to their subordinates is that they fail to realize the underlying requirements for a sound delegation of authority. First, there must be a statement of the objectives expected of an individual before authority can be well defined. Without this it is difficult to tell what kind of authority a man should have.

Second, and most critically, there must be an arrangement at the end of the period for holding the man soundly accountable for the total accomplishment of that objective weighed against the total cost of all errors incurred. Without accountability, authority leads to chaos. Managers are often disappointed in the judgment exercised by subordinates because accountability has not been set up before giving a man authority. Decentralization programs fail for this reason. *Accountability must precede authority.* And objectives alone do not necessarily assure accountability. The failure to recognize that accountability must be set up first is frequently the source of costly misdirection of effort down the line.

AUTHORITY FOR NEW PEOPLE

New employees present special authority problems, especially if you want them to develop rapidly. A firm may have been operating for some time with experienced people. Then new people replace them and the manager is surprised at the number of errors they make. He approaches the problem quite logically in view of his experience. He begins to believe that he just cannot depend on the quality of the people he gets now. People have changed. He therefore feels that he cannot allow any leeway on new jobs. Waste goes up, output suffers, and basic results are poor. . . . These problems very frequently occur because authority is not fully understood as it applies to new employees.

When you view authority as the amount of error that would be permitted in the light of the normal decisions expected of the man, it becomes clear that these normal decisions are not the same for a new person as they are for an experienced one. In other words, *both the objectives expected and the authority limits that go with them should be less when the person is new.* As the man gradually works in, both the objectives expected of him and the authority that you give him should be expanded. In other words, he should learn to crawl before he walks. When this is done well, the employee works in much more quickly, acquiring confidence and a sound sense of accountability as he moves along, without a feeling that he just cannot make the grade. At the same time the supervisor is in control of the operation.

Many new employees lose heart before they have given the job a chance. One of the prime reasons is that the supervisor assumed that they should have the same authority that the previous, more experienced people had. A great deal of waste and quite a few errors often result, along with a strong feeling of personal inadequacy on the part of the new person. The breaking-in period becomes much longer than would normally be the case. Although the tendency is to blame the new employee, the problem often stems from an overdelegation of authority to him in the beginning.

Management people fail for this reason, often capable management people. It is frequently assumed that a new man (new to the job, even though he has had much experience) should immediately make the same kinds of decisions that the long-experienced, proven man had made before him. This assumption imposes an extremely difficult problem in encouraging the new man to go ahead without stubbing his toe. He may make a decision which develops into a major error. He knows full well that a major error is not easily forgotten. He may have difficulty afterward both in retaining his own confidence and in retaining the confidence of his superior in his ability to act.

He therefore does not actually **feel** that he can make decisions that may result in errors. The overdelegation of authority to new men has important implications in the development of management personnel as lower-echelon people are promoted. On the higher job, in effect, the man is new.

6

Policies That Stimulate Individual Initiative

As an institution settles down after its inception, it is natural for a manager to sit back and review the inadequacies of past operations. He is usually struck by incidents that appear to him to point up a lack of cohesiveness indicated by a tendency toward repetition of mistakes. Men in charge of any enterprise work toward the development of some kind of code or central approach in a desire to create more order out of what appears to be chaos. They attempt to reduce the lesson of past happenings into some mode of acceptable operation that will develop this order in the future. Their interpretation of order usually means the prevention of all past aberrations, losses, or errors, a natural and logical move and one that is often very helpful. However, in doing this they often fail to recognize that human enterprise is generally best served by a series of trials resulting in deviations or errors which cumulatively develop greater insight and intuition in the individual. Greater creativity and substantially greater accomplishment are the result.

A typical outcome of this kind of "ordered" thinking in most institutions is the development of policy. It seems logical to a manager that he develop specific policies which will prevent the errors and deviations that he observed in the past. Unfortunately, these policies often go too far. They can easily tend to be restrictive—to discourage real accomplishment rather than encourage it. They may fail to recognize that all individuals grow and learn to a large extent by trial and error. Such errors must be accepted as part of normal operation.

To start out with, *policies should be looked at as a form of authority definition.* In most cases they limit the leeway or freedom of action of an individual at a lower echelon. These limitations should be minimal, only what is absolutely necessary to maintain the major direction of the enterprise. The difficulty arises, however, in trying to determine what is absolutely necessary. It is helpful as a guide to view policy as a means to encourage men to exercise sound judgment rather than one to discourage them. Policy should be viewed as an aid in further clarifying the extreme limits on the authority to be granted. Normally, this clarification forbids certain types of actions which over a period of time would consistently lead away from the general acceptable trend of the enterprise.

One difficulty with policies in many institutions is that they tend to cover detailed procedure—the "how to do it."

They fail to *differentiate between policy and detailed procedure.* This differentiation affords one critical check of the soundness of the policy. Procedure is something that follows after a policy has been determined. The more detailed the procedure, the more it limits the leeway of the individual. A clear example of such a limitation is the detailed procedure usually set up in government offices or in large companies. Wherever possible, procedures should be determined at as low a level as possible.

Unexplained policy can be just as restrictive as detailed policy. Since it is helpful to look at policy as a form of authority definition, it should be scrutinized for its possible effect on the individual's feeling of freedom to take action. Ordinarily, an unexplained policy is difficult to understand or interpret. To play safe the individual may interpret it much more narrowly than was intended by the superior. This is particularly true if something once goes wrong and he is criticized for it even though he had interpreted his action as being within policy. The area in which the individual will make decisions is therefore constricted. In effect his authority is reduced. For example, unexplained employee relations policy often results in inaction on the part of supervisors, particularly if a union represents the employees.

Since *policy* is really a limitation on authority, it *must be realistic in view of present conditions.* It must be reviewed for change whenever conditions change. For example, when a firm adds a new product line, present sales policy may be inapplicable because of the different customers, different areas, or different forms of distribution involved. There is a tendency for the firm to try to apply its former sales policy directly to the new product-merchandising program. This may strap the growth of the new product line.

What should be the purpose of policy? An effective approach is: *Policy should be looked upon as giving corporate or departmental "intent."* In any organized effort every individual experiences difficulty in grasping the over-all direction of the thinking of the institution. If he once understands the general mode of thinking and the reason "why," he can usually make fairly good judgments in regard to problems that face him. Policies can then be broader. It becomes increasingly unnecessary to define policy in detail or to develop detailed procedures. The man is encouraged toward wider experimentation and more risk taking in making decisions. At the same time, paradoxically enough, he tends to keep closer to the intended direction of the enterprise.

In order to clarify the difference between policy and procedure it is very often helpful to differentiate between them. Policy should normally give the intent. Procedure (where necessary) should dictate specific steps that should be followed in order to recognize the policy. An excellent method of highlighting this is to issue a two-sided sheet. On the left is the policy, on the right the procedure that exemplifies the policy (see Figure 4). The intent of the policy is therefore highlighted, often leading to a reduction in the necessary procedures that go with it. In addition, such an analysis points up the inadequacies of procedures that may have been first accepted as if they were policies and seem now to be somewhat immutable.

Since policies are aimed at giving intent and in a general

way at giving the employee the continuous direction of thinking of the institution, it becomes clear that long-range objectives are necessary. *Policies should fit the needs of long-range objectives.* Policies themselves are difficult to formulate adequately unless long-range objectives have

Policy	Procedure
1. Quality shall meet that of principal competitors	1. All products shall be checked by the Quality Department on a sample basis according to engineering standards set by the Development Department
2. Pay shall be an incentive to better work, more important work, or more work	2. Each employee's performance shall be reviewed by his superior for salary purposes every six months
3. All merchandising shall be through distributor organization	3. No direct sales shall be made to dealers. All home office sales shall be credited to the distributor in the area of the purchaser
4. All employees must be made accountable for any exercise of authority	4. All deviations from budget shall be reviewed by the immediate supervisor

FIG. 4 Policy *vs.* procedure.

first been developed. For example, it is difficult to have sound product development policies without having long-range objectives for product development. Failure to appreciate this requirement is a frequent error in policy formation. The policy formulators have not first determined the basic company or departmental objectives that make the policy necessary. Long-range objectives highlight which policies are absolutely necessary or helpful and act to *hold policies down to a reasonable number*. Whenever the number of policies is held within reasonable limits, it becomes easier for the individual under policy to operate effectively and utilize his own imagination. There is a distinct limit to the number of policies that any individual seems able to bear in mind realistically when making decisions. Beyond a certain point, policies merely create fear that some violation is occurring. One of the common expressions of this phenomenon is the oft-repeated phrase, "We can't do it; it's against company policy."

7

Accountability Must Be Personal

A SUPERIOR may have exercised a great deal of care in defining the objectives for an individual. In addition, policy may be well laid out and authority reasonably well defined. But somehow things do not get done as expected. Costs grow. There is a tendency for a man to disclaim blame for problems that occur. Activities lag that should have kept up to schedule. At times the individual engages in activities which contribute little if anything to the objectives of the enterprise. . . . There is an inclination on the part of the superior to view these occurrences as indications of an employee's lack of interest or moral fiber. In many cases, this is an erroneous conclusion. These may all be symptoms of a lack of a sound system of accountability. Individual accountability has not found its way down into the individual feelings of the employee.

What Is Accountability?

Basically, accountability means this: *If an objective is delegated to a man, he must* ***feel*** *a sense of obligation for its accomplishment.* If it is accomplished, he, personally, will be given full credit for it. If it is not, he knows that he will get the discredit. Note the implication of the word "feel." Accountability is meaningless until it gets down to the personal feelings of the individual. The man must feel that it applies to him and no one else. This is forgotten by many executives in their wish to adhere to a democratic principle. Committee meetings, coordinators, and communications are usually poor substitutes.

A manager may assume that if he delegates responsibility for a result, accomplishment will automatically be assured. This is not true. The man concerned must also feel accountability for the result. It is helpful to differentiate between these two aspects of the question. In general, delegation for responsibility is a downward process from a manager to a subordinate. The manager is stating what he wants the subordinate to accomplish. Accountability indicates the sense of obligation for accomplishment of the results going upward from the subordinate to the superior. It is a different process (see Figure 5). To be most effective, however, the procedure for establishing accountability should be set up at the same time that the original delegation is established, a point that is often lost sight of.

In a simplified way you may say that the major job of a manager is to get each of his men to assume personal accountability for the section of expected company results assigned to him. In essence, the man must assume the obligation to get these results. He must accept accountability for both positive and negative results; otherwise responsibility merely becomes a word. Accountability is the very lifeblood of an organization. It is generally the basis on which a manager must build in order to stimulate his people to sound accomplishment. Results are not usually accomplished fully without accountability, and accountability is meaningless unless it is reinforced by some kind of personal reward or penalty for the individual concerned.

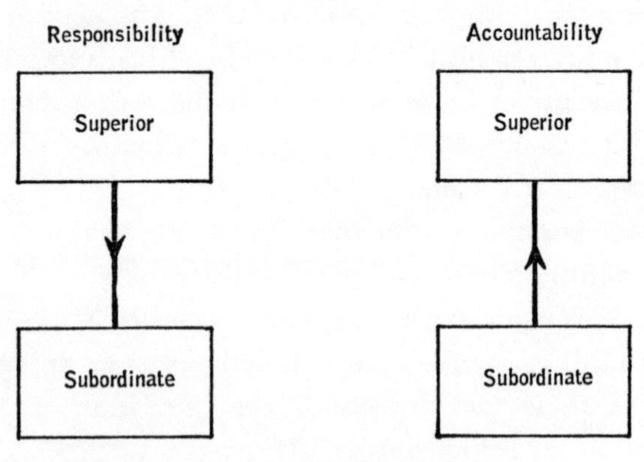

FIG. 5 Responsibility-accountability flow.

Compensation is a fertile area for forcing accountability. A management plan that does not tie the results that have been defined into pay is usually missing a prime spur to accountability. In our economy money is viewed as an indication of value contributed. To the employee, salary increases and bonuses are usually taken as symbols of acceptable performance.

On the other hand, salary raises given routinely at the end of every year without regard to personal accomplishment imply no accountability for results. Pay should be viewed as incentive—incentive toward more accomplishment, better accomplishment, or continuation of accomplishment. It should be geared to the objectives that have been set for the man, whether it be in salary or in bonus. The more it is tied to factors other than these, the more it weakens accountability.

The same thing applies to any appraisal of the employee—implying as it does the supervisor's approval or criticism of the man's action. Appraisals in some firms are based on traits such as judgment, initiative, ingenuity; or on action such as cooperation, coordination, or planning. These may have little relationship to sound accomplishment. To the employee they often, therefore, appear unfair and unpredictable. In addition, it is often difficult to get uniformity in interpretation. Appraisals should be geared to the results expected of the man. To the extent that they are not, the employee will not feel personally accountable—a perfectly natural reaction—because, in fact, he is able to make a good impression without the accomplishment of results.

The same holds true of the various other ways of recognizing individuals: promotions, commendations, special benefits, etc. Frequently length of service carries too much weight. Unless these rewards are given as far as possible in the light of accomplishment of results, point by point the employee feels relieved of a feeling of personal accountability for the results that are expected of him. To that extent you do not develop a company-minded employee working consistently toward the results expected.

The man concludes that other things count more than accomplishment. Political intrigue is likely to start within an operation.

The Basis for Accountability

Some employees acquire a strong feeling of professional pride about their work. They feel that their activity is more important than the specific accomplishment expected by the company. With other employees, departmental loyalties override company loyalty, with the net effect that people are working toward departmental consolidation (and growth) rather than toward profitable company results. At times their work may actually negate the constructive work of others. When these things occur, it is very often due to a failure to make each man accountable for his portion of the over-all result of the enterprise. Instead, he has been made accountable for activity. He has been able to satisfy his superior by presenting a long list of things he did with little specific emphasis on their total consequences.

Activity emphasis can be a prime problem with professional people. They may hide behind the cloak of "professionally sound" actions and describe all the standard procedures and actions they have gone through, even though little or no net contribution to the company has resulted. For example, a product development man may feel that he has done a superb job by testing one material after another. He may therefore feel that no one should hold him personally accountable for the fact that he has developed no new products.

An accountant may call attention to the fine statements that he has presented. He may be especially proud of their completeness (10 extra pages). He may stress the fact that all expense is allocated; everything is covered. At the same time he is taken aback if you ask him what these statements accomplished for the money spent developing them, or if just as much accomplishment could have been realized in managing the business with reports one-half the size. He may have difficulty understanding what you mean, because he has not been made accountable for making a contribution to company results.

In both these cases a man has been allowed to avoid personal accountability for results and substitute for it an accountability for activity. Generally a weaker operation evolves and a poorly developed man as well. Some excellent men have been misguided simply by being held accountable only for activity over a period of time.

It is often erroneously assumed that the sound definition of responsibility within a company means that a result is assigned to one man and that he alone will affect the accomplishment of that result—the doctrine of "unique accountability." In actual practice this kind of situation almost never occurs. Almost all enterprise is really cooperative enterprise. In practice you almost always find that two or more people actually affect a result. *If a man has a strong influence on a result, he must be held accountable for it, even though other people may also have some effect on that result.* This rule is merely a recognition of the practicalities of business operation. No one ever has "full" authority. What we are really saying is that nobody will ever have complete control of the result for which he is held accountable. To some extent the statement that a man must operate within the general policies of the company is an example of this. If a man exercises a considerable influence, however—by action, by memoranda, by record setups, by control of timing, or in any other way—he must be held accountable for the negative or positive effects of this influence. Without this kind of accountability, operations end in chaos.

In some firms antagonisms develop between men. One man feels the other is not contributing. Perhaps a man develops a little empire and no one else knows what is going on except that he constantly requests more help. Frequently this results from a lack of accountability for results that blend in with the over-all results expected of the firm. He therefore feels he can impress his superior by the very size of his activity. (In justice to him, salary plans often encourage this by giving too much emphasis to the number of subordinates or activities supervised instead of to results accomplished.)

Error Accountability Is Not Results Accountability

There are some people who always seem to be afraid to move. They may have a tendency to cover up almost any error that occurs. They are generally content to wait until somebody above gives the nod before they take any action. When action is finally taken, it is often too late to prevent major losses. In an attempt to overcome these problems daily meetings develop in order to keep on top of all the little difficulties which seem to be occurring and which are not solved. . . . Very often this whole situation is the result of a poor accountability setup. It commonly stems from a basic mistake made by many supervisors, that of focusing on errors and not on over-all results in holding a man accountable.

Here is how it may develop. A man goes ahead and makes a decision which turns out badly. His supervisor hears about it and discusses the error with him (in a perfectly natural attempt to prevent the same error from occurring again). To the man this is a criticism. It is extremely difficult for the supervisor to point out an error in this way without having the employee feel that he has lost status in the eyes of his superior. (I am assuming, of course, that this error was supposedly within the authority of the man.) In the future this man tends to cover up or hesitate to make any decisions on any similar item before he asks his supervisor.

There are added implications when the man faces a problem that is just a little bit different from those of the past. He may be so afraid of making an error that he will not move. By focusing on specific errors, the supervisor has violated the Rule of Errors defined on page 48 and, in effect, taken back authority.

The supervisor must apply the exception principle. In other words, only the exceptionally large error or an exceptionally large number of errors (beyond the man's authority in either case) should be called to the superior's attention for his personal review with the employee. His action is then consistent with the Rule of Errors. But the man must be accountable at the end of the period for total results and total cost of all errors. Many people have paid lip service to the exception principle without recognizing its true meaning and its implications in dealing with an individual employee. Its important meaning comes from an acceptance of a sound approach to the over-all accountability of the employee. It cannot be applied without such an approach.

Creative Results First—then Cost

Many companies with well-developed accounting records or budgets have had the disappointing experience of finding that although their cost standards are almost always met, cost trends do not substantially improve. New improvements are not put into effect. Sales volume does not grow and the company does not expand rapidly. Modern methods are not eagerly grasped and installed. This situation may occur when, in effect, people are made accountable for costs first and for results afterward (if at all). For example, excessive focus on inventory turnover in a supermarket (control of cost of inventory) can easily lead to bare shelves and fewer sales.

A man may get the feeling that he is doing his job very well as long as he keeps within his budget. In actual practice, he may not be putting in the improvements that he should. He may be using every trick possible either to raise the budget initially (such as using up an unneeded budget so he won't be cut in the next period) or to dump extra cost and effort onto somebody else. He is actually encouraged to let certain results slip so that he will show up well against the budget.

Frequently excessive pressure on costs has deleterious

long-run effects. It may emphasize the short run over the long run. Cost reduction programs have often erred in this regard. In overemphasizing costs almost to the exclusion of accomplishment, they have developed a lack of accountability for creative results. At times companies have been seriously retarded for years afterward. For example, such a cost reduction program may result in the elimination of a percentage of indirect employees (such as staff or supervisory employees). There may very well be too many, but making a percentage across-the-board cut in their numbers very often results in poorly balanced operations and in a lack of accountability for real results. In many cases each supervisor and staff man remaining may then be expected to accomplish far more than is humanly possible. He tends to let things slide. As a consequence, the company suffers in the future, with sloppy operation being accepted as normal. In one plant where this type of cost cutting was effected, unit cost gradually increased 15 per cent in four or five years because of inadequate staff help and supervision. The financial statement had indicated an immediate sharp reduction in cost, however.

Accountability Before Authority

In some supposedly "liberally" administered companies executives lean over backward to give people leeway. (This is particularly true of certain relatively inexperienced executives.) Employees feel free to take almost any action they wish. There is no hesitancy on the part of one man to step into another man's bailiwick. People are free in their criticism of other people and are constantly making suggestions about the work of the other fellow. At the same time their own work may suffer. Frequently heavy losses are occurring in relatively minor jobs. . . . Very often this situation is a reflection of a major organizational error, the granting of authority before accountability has been firmly set up.

A man must be made accountable before he is granted any authority. It is chaos to give authority before a man is made firmly accountable. A common violation of this rule occurs with salesmen and sales managers. In many firms they, in effect, determine prices by exercising a strong influence toward cutting prices so that they can sell more easily. But they may not be held accountable for the impact on net profit resulting from cutting prices! In that event they should have no authority to reduce price. They may be given authority, however (and quite profitably for the firm), if they are held accountable in some way for the effect of their actions on profit (for total sales profit realized from their accounts, for example).

A firm may get requests for considerable outlays of money for machinery, equipment, methods, or almost any kind of expense, especially for research and development projects. The people making these requests may feel no personal accountability if the money spent does not result in a sound return for the company. It is extraordinary how much more careful they are about making requests when they know that they will be personally called on the carpet if the projects do not pay off. Such accountability also forces better planning of projects so that the money is more effectively spent when it is granted.

Without Measurement, No Accountability

Many firms find their people becoming satisfied with mediocre operation. Men become relaxed to the point of an easy existence. Sometimes important results are lagging, with heavy cost, and nobody seems enough concerned about it to take strong and timely action. . . . This condition often develops because too little effort has been made to measure the results that should be expected of each and every key person in the firm.

You cannot have a "results" accountability without measurement! The time and effort spent to get even an estimated measurement, a crude measurement, or an over-all measurement is well worthwhile to provide a basis for tying in accountability. Frequently men will say that certain activities are not measurable. In our opinion, if they are not measurable (either short-range or long-range), the chances are there is very little there to measure and it is highly questionable whether the job is necessary. In the end every function must in some way show a result which will favorably affect the objectives of the enterprise. Surely there was originally some idea in someone's mind as to the achievement that was expected when setting up the position! It is only through a system of measurement that real accountability can be forcefully maintained and driven home to each individual.

Measurement is a vital necessity in determining the need for a job. It is difficult to organize soundly without it. Jobs multiply and grow and departments increase. Positions develop and are maintained for years before it is discovered that they are not needed any more. Such an occurrence usually means that there has been no continuing attempt to measure the results that should be expected from the job and then to lead from this to accountability for the individual. This failing is common in firms that have defined positions by activity—common especially in laboratories where maturity curves are emphasized in salary administration. The setup implies that no measurement need be made of the final effect on the enterprise and tends to prevent sound accountability.

Men have difficulty focusing on results unless there is a measurement that can lead to accountability. You do not necessarily get improvement along with salary increases unless you have measurement tied to accountability. Instead you get a focus on activity, on action, or on various phases of work without necessarily getting a definite advance toward the objectives of the enterprise. In our estimation, measurement is a necessity if you wish to develop each management person into a farsighted, broad-thinking, contributing member of the management team. He needs measurement of his results to begin to think from a management point of view. He has to know specifically where he stands. A method for measurement should be part of an organization design to get the most results.

8

Special Characteristics of Groups

As THE WORK demand increases, more men may be needed. The supervisor must delegate to a number of people doing the same or similar work. Because of the similarity of the work done, there is a tendency to treat individuals as duplicates or machines to be manipulated by the superior. The supervisor may fail to recognize that a man is an emotional being and not ordinarily subject to strict engineering planning. Frequently he does not take into account individual differences between men. Relationships between individuals also cause difficulties. Supervision, therefore, becomes more complicated. To meet this complication, however, there is a tendency to substitute procedure for supervision. Less reliance may be placed on the judgment of the individual. As a consequence he does not grow.

Make It a Full Job

A supervisor may discover that when he has a group of men, on the average they produce less. Soldiering on the job creeps in. A slower pace is accepted as normal operation. For example, suppose a department has a considerable fluctuation in its work load depending on the time of the year or the time of the month, so that at times there are only five hours of work to do in a normal eight-hour work period. A man quite naturally tends to stretch out the five hours of work into eight hours. He automatically develops a slower pace. A supervisor may accept this pace, rationalizing that when a rush period comes he, the supervisor, is going to be more demanding. Human beings do not readily adjust in this way, however. We are all creatures of habit. The man is much more likely to hold to the same pace in the rush period and feel that he is overworked. He will believe that more men should be hired or more overtime put in. The net effect is that the slow pace of the five-hour work period becomes accepted as normal. The difficulty may be compounded in a government office that is overmanned. Reducing the manpower usually means reducing the number of employees in different classifications. Even key employees are affected, so they, too, resist as long as there is money in the budget.

What is the normal inclination of a salesman who has sold what is considered a month's sales by the twentieth of the month? He may have done a very good selling job, but he may also have had some unusual conditions that made sales easy. He is inclined to relax from then on! The net effect is that the total volume is considerably less than what could have been achieved.

In order to maintain high effort, the supervisor must make sure that he spends enough time laying out the work so that each man has a full job every day of the week and every week of the year. Objectives may have to be better planned. In some cases this may mean planning for fill-in work. In other cases it may mean a reliance on part-time employees. It is the responsibility of a supervisor to plan as far as possible in a way that minimizes the ups and downs on each job which could lead the employee to feel that he hasn't a full job to do. Otherwise men develop a false impression of a full day's (week's, or month's) work and begin to accept partial application as normal. This is a common cause of an excessive number of personnel developing in office and staff positions as the company grows. Featherbedding often starts in the same way, and the firm gets less output per man. Management is inclined to blame the attitude of the employees, but in many cases the cause is faulty supervisory planning.

Use Full Skill

A related problem occurs when the work that a supervisor requires of his men is quite variable in the skill required. Both simple and highly skilled work are required of the same job. Suppose only 15 per cent of the work on a job is highly skilled. Pay is usually in line with the highest skill required. In this case, the supervisor is not getting a full day's work out of the skill that he is paying for. But there are further implications. A highly skilled man tends to take less interest in nonskilled work. To him it offers no challenge. For instance, in technical jobs highly trained technical people may be asked to do simple checking work. The highly skilled man often does a poorer job on the low-skilled work than a low-skilled employee would do, even though he is overpaid for it. He is not interested in the work, and he becomes dissatisfied.

Underutilization of skill often develops under the banner of flexibility. It is natural for a supervisor to want a setup where any employee could do any of the work. Flexibility has tremendous appeal. It may be very costly, however, resulting in a very high payroll for the total work being done. Highly skilled employees may also become dissatisfied. A hospital may suffer in this way, but a solution lies in having more of the nurses' routine work taken over by nurse's aides. The technical skill of the nurse is then better utilized and the work is done more cheaply.

The supervisor may be well advised to divide up the work by skills even though all phases of the job could be done by one man. Perhaps he can organize the work into two or more jobs, one of relatively simple duties and one of more complex tasks. There may be an added advantage in that such a setup provides a better means of training in new people and making them pay their way early. A word of caution, however! In breaking up the work the supervisor should make sure that he is providing a full job for each person continuously so that poor habits of work accountability are not encouraged. In addition, each person should still be held accountable for a definable result. Otherwise costs may go up.

Authority for Each Member

A supervisor sometimes has difficulty adjusting himself to the over-all authority requirement that he is delegating to his group. He may forget that authority is an individual thing. Although he may have willingly granted a certain amount of authority to one man, he is often disinclined to delegate that same amount to each of several employees working for him. As a consequence, his people are constantly coming to him for decisions. He becomes a "crutch." Because of his failure to delegate authority soundly, he finds that he is constantly in on day-to-day and hour-to-hour problems.

Authority delegation is even more difficult at higher management levels. As a man advances he has to adjust himself to a wider and wider concept of the authority to be delegated to his subordinates. As we stated earlier, authority means the freedom to make errors. In this case, then, it means the freedom to make large errors. Because of this failure to delegate adequate authority, the superior discovers that he cannot get other key people to take action he believes he used to take when he was doing that work. "They just don't seem to take responsibility." It is hard for him to realize that much of this is his own fault.

At any level in the operation the supervisor's approach to authority should be similar to that described in Chapter 5, page 49. His tendency, however, is to be tighter than he was when he had just one man and to limit the leeway he is allowing. Each subordinate should have as much authority as he needs to make decisions up to the place where his work affects others. Policy starts to come in at this point. A prime purpose of policy is to provide a necessary degree of uniformity of purpose between individual members of a group. Each supervisor should view the broader development of uniform policy as part of the authority definition for his group. It is, in effect, a type of standard authority definition.

Records Become Stimulators

Records have an added effect on the authority of a group. A supervisor's natural tendency is to have all records come to him. This is the way to keep informed! (Chief executives gravitate naturally to this philosophy.) Such a procedure leads automatically to a centralization of decision making and to a retarding of the development of subordinates. The consequence is either that employees are not excessively concerned about their problems or that the production of poorer members of the group becomes par for the group. There is also a tendency for over-all records of groups to hide individual deviations instead of pointing them up to the individual man so that he can take corrective action.

When all the records come to the supervisor, he tends to give out only that information which seems to him at the time to be especially apropos. He fails to recognize that this is not the way to stimulate a sense of accountability in the individual. The man has to know the whole story. Sometimes the centralization of information is carried on under the guise of confidentiality—information is considered highly secret (even though it is readily available to anyone interested enough to do a little checking).

For best results, ***each*** *man should know how he is doing compared to his objectives.* Group information is not adequate. Records should be devised by operation or by individual unit, whether it be in manufacturing, engineering, office, or sales. They should be current and provide a means of letting the individual employee know when there is an error that needs correcting. Either this information should be provided for the man, or he should have a means of recording it for himself. Such a record program should be part of the basic organizational setup to get the most effectiveness from each man in the group.

A supervisor is often reluctant to carry out this approach on records. It may appear burdensome. Ordinarily the increased accomplishment that is realized is much greater than the cost of the records. For that matter, since deviation need only be interpreted roughly in many cases, the cost is usually not great anyway.

Broaden the Planning

In supervising a group it may seem difficult to stay on top of all the ups and downs in work and to keep everybody profitably busy all the time. There seem to be frequent crises that are not easy to plan for.

One of the basic jobs of a supervisor is to organize so that he can plan the work of his people to get around these conditions. His job is changing, now that he has a number of people to direct. Unfortunately many supervisors look at this responsibility as a secondary part of their job. It is one of the major reasons why new supervisors fail to accomplish as much as was hoped from their group.

Define Decisions Retained by the Supervisor

There is a natural inclination for any supervisor to feel that he wants to clear with all "interested" parties—to follow the democratic process. He may be inclined this way because of the harsh comments frequently made against autocrats. This attitude can easily lead to an excessive number of meetings to "inform," however. A supervisor must recognize that there are some over-all problems on which he alone must make a decision and that the decision will be autocratic. He may get suggestions and advice from members of his group or from others, but he alone must make the decision. Otherwise decisions may become loose, and he will not be recognized as a leader. Which are the decisions best made by the supervisor? In the main they are those that cover the over-all group. Decisions affecting the day-to-day work of one individual should be so delegated that the man on the job can take action on them wherever possible.

Establish Sound Supervision

A supervisor may find that his people are making too many errors, and he just has not enough time to straighten them out. He is constantly running around putting out fires. In addition, his men may have trouble meeting reasonable schedules, and it takes a long time to break in new people. New programs lag; people do not apply themselves and push ahead as he had expected that they would. . . . These conditions are typical where there is a failure to recognize that *supervision is a major responsibility.*

A group of people working in a department are thinking, feeling human beings. As we said earlier, they cannot be handled as if they were just machines. It takes time to supervise them, to work with them, to stimulate them. If this is not done, the operation tends to suffer. Sound management design must provide adequate time for supervision.

What are the requirements of good supervision?

1. ***The supervisor must set up objectives.*** Employees are more effective when they know exactly what is expected of them in a particular period. They react well to such direction. However, it takes time to determine sound objectives which coordinate with other objectives. The supervisor must sit down with each employee and come to a complete understanding as to what is expected of him. The supervisor must provide this time; it is one of his key responsibilities.

2. ***The supervisor must train his people.*** Most people are willing to do a good job if they know what is expected of them and if they know how to do it. One of the grave errors of many supervisors is that they regard training as a routine job. As a consequence many parts of the job may be missed. Training is a prime responsibility of a supervisor at any level. It is essential that the supervisor makes sure that it is done completely, accurately, and effectively.

Without good training, new men may make a great many errors and retain poor habits for years afterward. The requirement of training is not usually satisfied by simply turning new people over to a senior man. Frequently the senior men are not good trainers. They are usually not interested in training a new man in every important facet of the job. Because they are not accountable for the total work of the trainee there are almost always gaps in the training they give. The man being trained may, therefore, not advance as rapidly as he should to a high plateau of performance.

3. ***The supervisor must develop men.*** Any firm must provide for replacements on key jobs and for promotions in periods of expansion. People learn best by doing, by being guided, and by being accountable on a job. The most effective development of a man comes through his supervisor. Special development courses are, at best, only an aid to this basic development. But it generally requires time and patience for the supervisor to assign work that will allow the man to exercise judgment and thus develop himself; to delegate assignments that will result in this self-development.

4. ***The supervisor must check and follow up*** on his people. People may make errors. They may go off in different directions because of misunderstanding. The supervisor, however, must develop some plan whereby he checks periodically. He may plan check points along the way. Otherwise people may repeat errors continually with high waste or poor result, and somehow errors never seem to get corrected. People may continually apply poor methods, but he does not discover it until a long time later. Delega-

tion without follow-up may be abdication of responsibility. The problem is magnified if many employees are new on their jobs.

Much of the follow-up has to be done in a fairly personal way to be sure that misunderstanding is minimized. However, the follow-up should not be carried on with an experienced man to the point where minor errors within the man's authority are scrutinized and commented on. On such a basis, the follow-up will hold the man back from making decisions. The follow-up on management people particularly must not constrict authority limits which must be broad enough to permit the man to make necessary decisions.

5. ***The supervisor must discipline*** his people. No one likes to take another person to task for some infraction. It is a nasty business at best. In addition, many people like a democratic process where we all get together and agree on something. It is inescapable, however, that a certain amount of autocracy is necessary in order to get effective operation. If an employee carries out loose practices or does things that interfere with other employees, someone must take him to task—usually his supervisor. Any cooperative enterprise needs laws. The supervisor must, in effect, police these laws. In this regard, restrictions such as civil service regulations and some union contract clauses may present a major obstacle to good supervision because of the time-consuming hearings and possible political reprisals that may face a conscientious supervisor trying to do his job.

6. ***The supervisor must stimulate*** his people. Human beings do not react like machines. They are thinking individuals, feeling individuals. They react well to attention.

They can develop fears, hesitations, and lose interest. A slow tempo may result and quality may go down. Stimulating his people is a day-to-day and hour-to-hour job for each supervisor but one that can easily go by default in the press of other work.

People react well to a pat on the back. It is sometimes difficult for a supervisor to recognize this in the case of his subordinates even though he recognizes it as applied to himself. Supervisors may be inclined to say, "The man should know everything is all right unless I say otherwise." Perhaps this is true, but the fact remains that people produce more when they are constantly encouraged, whether they be vice-presidents or sweepers.

7. *The supervisor must install new methods.* There seems to be a natural inclination on the part of all employees to oppose new methods. This may be partly due to their previous experience. An employee who is settled in a comfortable rut may fear that the new method will require considerable change in his procedures. Or he may fear that it will endanger his position. Therefore, without a push for improvement, new methods generally do not move. Efficiency stays the same year in and year out, or perhaps even decreases.

We want to emphasize, however, that the supervisor should **install** new methods. The setup must encourage the supervisor to get ideas from anyone. It is his job to get them into operation. He should receive full credit no matter where he "steals" the ideas (from his own group or from outside his own group). A number of executives actually retard improvement by trying to differentiate between new ideas that the supervisor developed himself and those that he got from others. It should make no difference. In fact, an attempt to differentiate in this way is one of the surest ways to retard improvement.

8. Finally, ***the supervisor must call his people to account.*** In order to stimulate people soundly in the right direction, they must have the feeling that they get the complete credit or discredit if a result is or is not accomplished—they must have a sense of accountability. Its absence encourages laxity. Trouble spots remain and frequently poor workers are not discovered until after they have been on the job 5, 10, or 15 years.

As far as possible, accountability must be complete. If the supervisor weakly allows the employee an "out," he will have a poorer operation. You can readily see that the supervisor must first clearly and carefully set up objectives for each man so that he can later call him to account.

These requirements of good supervision should be part of the design of every supervisor's job. He should recognize them as primary responsibilities of his position. To the extent that he does not, he will get poorer operation from his group. He will not get the same results from each man that he would have expected from his close experience with just one man on the job.

Each supervisor should approach his job with the feeling that it is his function "to make the man successful." It is not his function simply to hold people to account for accountability's sake or to set up objectives just to see what they can do. He should be interested in getting each person to achieve the results that are expected. Every supervisor and executive should develop this philosophy throughout his entire operation.

9

Managing from the Second Management Echelon

When the work multiplies so greatly that one supervisor cannot coordinate it, several supervisors must be set up, each in charge of a group even though the work of all subordinates is similar (see Figure 6). The manager over all the groups is now more removed from the scene of action. He must rely on accomplishment through other supervision than his own. He must consider different approaches to communications, further refinement of delegation, and also methods for holding supervisors accountable. It becomes much more difficult to maintain a uniform effort throughout the operation.

Idle time may develop because groups are too large. Or one group may be dependent upon another, and there is a tendency for one "eager beaver" to try to show up another

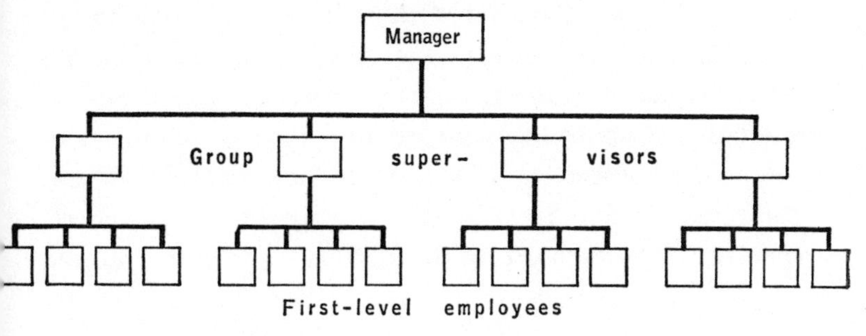

FIG. 6 Managing from the second management echelon.

supervisor instead of working with him. The delegations from a manager to a supervisor may not be broad enough to permit a redelegation by the supervisor. The manager must adjust his thinking to meet these problems.

Delegate by Major Sections of a Result

The manager must first delineate the specific results expected of each supervisor and also define a breadth of decision making that permits the supervisor to delegate specific results and adequate authority to his men. The manager should try to break up his own results into major semi-independent sections and assign a major section to each of his supervisors. Otherwise the requirement for careful personal coordination on his part is tremendously increased. The individual supervisor on the job gradually develops an attitude that he should simply follow orders as demanded instead of assuming responsibility. As a consequence, considerably less than full value may be obtained from him and, in turn, from his men.

The manager should delegate by the group results ex-

pected of each supervisor. Otherwise it is difficult to get the supervisor to go ahead and assume responsibility. Supervisors may blame each other if there is a great deal of overlap in responsibilities without a careful definition of cooperative objectives. If a manager looks at the groups as part of a central pool instead of assigning a specific responsibility to each group through its supervisor, training or discipline may go by the board. The central pool approach is often mistakenly taken under the masthead of flexibility. It usually indicates that a manager has not analyzed the work carefully enough. On a three-shift operation, the foreman of each shift must be given the responsibility for the work of his shift. A setup that rotates crews but not the foreman tends to violate this rule. District sales managers must be in control of the salesmen in their district. A project engineer in a laboratory should control the engineers and lab people engaged in his project. To the extent that many strings are placed on this control they do not feel accountable. The work tends to lag, and men are not well trained.

A Supervisor Must Plan

We mentioned earlier that planning should always be included as an integral part of a result. People accomplish more under these circumstances. One of the most common violations of this rule occurs where there are several supervisors supervising the same kind of work. There is a strong tendency, then, for the manager to do the planning. One frequent consequence is a larger total group than is necessary, in order to take care of "emergencies." The individual supervisors do not take personal responsibility for meeting these emergencies. The manager finds that he must always step in to take care of them. Even with over-staffed groups, there will probably be bottlenecks in periods of high output requirements. Instead of feeling personally accountable, supervisors wait to be notified of the plan for meeting each specific problem. It is an easy out. Their groups develop looseness.

In a string of lumberyards a central office drew all the house plans for the yard managers. The managers only felt partially accountable for the plans and the sales that should have resulted. In addition, they made little effort to learn simple drafting so that they could give quicker service.

As far as possible, *planning the work of his group should be the responsibility of each supervisor.* He should be required to develop his own information grapevine in order to do his planning effectively. Where there is a day-to-day tie-in with other groups, he should be responsible for effectively carrying through on this tie-in. The design of his job must steer him in that direction. Only the plans for making major decisions or those covering the setup for relationships between the supervisors should be made by the manager.

There is a further problem when the manager does all the planning. Unfortunately he often does this on the basis of inadequate facts. The more removed a man is from the first line of operation, the more difficult it is for him to be aware of all the little problems involved in carrying through on a plan.

In essence each supervisor must be required to plan for the most effective contribution of his group toward the over-all plans envisioned by the manager. This rule applies just as much to district sales managers as it does to foremen or accounting supervisors. Each should plan ahead to effectively utilize the resources at his disposal in order to get the results expected of his group. Supervisors react well to this requirement. It is a major step in developing broad supervisors. They become better candidates for promotion to managerial positions. As a company or department grows there is a tendency to drift away from this requirement and centralize much of the planning. Sometimes this is helpful. Too often, however, it goes so far that the growth of supervisors is seriously retarded.

Make Cooperation Advantageous

Many managers assume that a "loyal" employee will naturally cooperate in projects that are best for the institution as they see it. When a man does not do this they take it as an indication of personal disloyalty. They fail to recognize that most people cooperate when they feel that it is to their personal advantage (not necessarily a financial advantage). When supervisors "pass the buck" and when they do not tackle difficult problems, a poor managerial setup may be at fault rather than a lack of willingness on the part of the management team to pitch in. If no one will admit personal responsibility for major errors and there is a tendency to assume that everybody had a hand in them, this too may be a reflection of a poor management setup. One group does not normally feel accountable for the failure of an activity unless that accountability has been clearly defined from the start.

Here we get to a variation of the "results" delegation that we discussed earlier (see Chapter 7, page 67). It is often assumed that any result can be assigned to only one man—that it is impossible to hold more than one person accountable for a result—the theory of unique accountability. Managers often feel that this applies especially to supervisors. In actual practice one rarely finds a result that is not dependent on the effective work of several people, especially when you get into supervisory and managerial jobs. Sound management operation, then, would hold each supervisor accountable for those results that his group could accomplish alone and, in addition, for results that will effectively aid other groups. Cooperative results must be reflected in his objectives. In other words, the supervisor must be accountable for results that require cooperation with other groups. Otherwise he will not delegate a responsibility for cooperation to his men.

Two foremen may be responsible for the same work on different shifts. There may be a great deal of carry-over on certain activities such as housekeeping, machine maintenance, and safety. If each foreman is not held accountable for the total result, he may tend to shove off this work on the other.

Two district sales managers may both influence a particular customer. In a railroad, one freight traffic supervisor may control contacts with the vendor, another with the receiver. The results expected of each of them must be so designed that both get credit for the consummation of this sale—both are accountable.

Designing cooperation into results delegation is a major requirement of sound management planning. Cooperation must be made to the mutual advantage of the individuals or groups concerned. This requirement pervades the management plan of almost any operation that has graduated from the stage of the very simplest delegation between two men. It is very frequently missed by executives in the slavish adherence to the principle of unique accountability. They fail to analyze what is necessary at the primary level to get the work done and then fail to set up a design that encourages necessary cooperation at each level above.

Retain Major Decisions Affecting All Groups

Some of a manager's supervisors may fight to get the easy work. Others may follow methods that make for difficult tie-in with other supervisors, so that it is hard to meet schedules at a reasonable cost. When responsibilities "float" and can't be pinned down to an individual supervisor, or when supervisors apply different policies, the manager's delegation should be analyzed. His method of holding supervisors accountable for cooperative results may cause these problems. The starting point is the review of his own responsibilities—which he should retain and which he should delegate.

The same general rule applies here as in simpler delegation. The manager should retain those responsibilities where the most value is at stake. In addition to this, however, he must retain those important decisions that affect all his supervisors and especially those that are necessary to develop cooperation. He should make the decisions on the ground rules for the relationship between his supervisors. If he leaves these decisions up to the supervisors affected, he invites weak operation. We do not mean that he should discourage one supervisor from talking over a problem with another and perhaps arriving at a mutually satisfactory conclusion without bothering the manager. The ground rules and cooperative objectives should encourage this on a day-to-day basis.

The manager must retain supervision of his supervisors but ordinarily delegate to the supervisor much of the responsibility for the methods involved in achieving results. It is only when these methods substantially affect the work of other supervisors that the manager may have to retain some of the responsibility.

A general sales manager may decide the general sales policies, approaches, and pricing that will affect all sales effort. In some cases he must decide which types of customers, which types of territories, and which industries should be focused on. He must make the decision on overall sales expectation (and then break it down for each district sales manager) on new product push. The carrying-out of the work in each district and the specific approaches to his customers must generally be decided, however, by the district sales manager, who should have the authority to do this.

A construction superintendent must make those decisions affecting all his supervisors. He must decide the broad assignment of results expected of each of the groups. He must decide policies on construction, on employees, on timing, etc., that would affect all the groups. He must also retain those decisions that delineate the results expected of one supervisor as against another and those that are necessary for cooperation between them. Within these policies and responsibility definitions each supervisor should make the current decisions necessary to get his results, up to the point where he impinges unreasonably on others. Beyond this point decisions would normally be made by the superintendent.

Overdelegation Is Costly

Because of his inclination toward a democratic process and the desire of his supervisors for more and more authority, a manager may actually overdelegate. Each supervisor wants to "run his own show." Overdelegation may lead to poor communication, to excessive payroll, and to imbalance in the operation. The manager may have poor control of the operation because he is removed from it. The individual supervisor may go too far in one direction.

Perhaps a manager (*A* in Figure 7) delegates all his responsibilities to just two supervisors (*B* and *C*). He feels that he is proving that he is a broad manager by delegating, forgetting that he should delegate only when the work is too much for him to do. Managing two men is probably

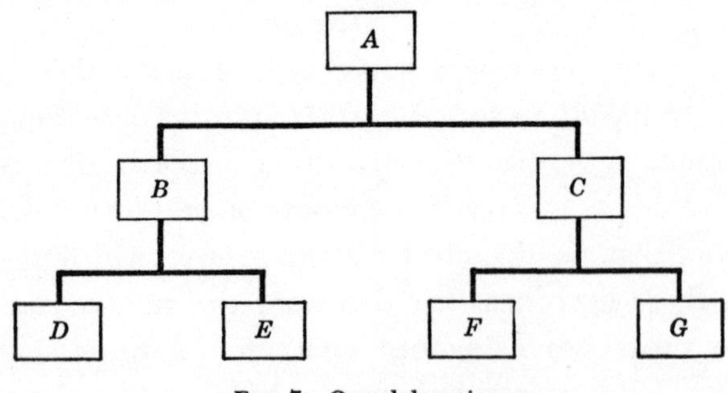

FIG. 7 Overdelegation.

not a full-time managerial job. The manager is not fully utilizing his own ability, because he could probably coordinate the work of five, six, or seven supervisors. His supervisors tend to follow his example and they in turn may each redelegate to just two men (*D* and *E; F* and *G*). The cost of administration goes up. The manager could probably have supervised *D, E, F,* and *G* directly himself.

Each of the extra levels probably adds a 20 or 25 per cent obstacle to communications. The manager finds himself more removed from the problems occurring at the first level, the place where the work is done. It is harder to get all the facts and relay his decisions downward.

Suppose that a manager does not have enough work to delegate most of his results to his supervisors and still have a full coordinating job himself. What should he do then? He should probably retain some of the direct supervision for himself and perhaps have only one subsupervisor rather than two or three. In this way he will make more effective use of his own abilities. The only sound reason for delegating is that the work is just too much or too difficult for the manager to do himself.

An accounting manager who has only two supervisors reporting to him is probably overdelegating. This overdelegation usually causes an overretention of the planning function because the accounting manager hasn't a full job to do. He also tends to inject himself into the day-to-day work of his supervisors. His supervisors do not develop well and he has poor control of the work. His supervisors are inclined to let him make the decisions (thereby proving to him the necessity for his constant interference). Since it seems so necessary and logical, the accounting manager finds it difficult to avoid making these decisions himself. He is merely perpetuating a poor situation.

In smaller companies a general sales manager may succumb to this same problem. Perhaps the sales force has grown to the point where he has 11 or 12 salesmen. He feels the need for help. His inclination is to set up another sales manager under him to supervise the 11 or 12 people —usually a poor mode of delegation at this stage. He will not capitalize fully on his own abilities, because there is not enough work for him to do over and above the supervision of the sales force. Because of this lack of work, he will be inclined to inject himself into the current problems of the salesmen. In addition, his assistant is not likely to develop so that he takes full responsibility for salesmen.

In larger companies the same difficulty often arises in the case of a branch manager. The lack of development of his men that results is often the reason for failure in promotions and for greater centralization of procedures.

COORDINATE THE WORK OF THE GROUPS

There are a number of specific problems that present themselves when a manager has to coordinate the work of several supervisors. The interrelationships and the problems of blending are more complex than they are when the delegation is directly to one group. In many cases, these interrelationships take much of the time of the manager.

Only One Supervisor for a Man

Any man tends to be less effective when he has more than one boss. The man is confused because he is not sure who his boss is, so he waits for instructions. It may take an inordinate amount of time for men to get thoroughly trained. Improvements may lag because improvement is now "nobody's" business. Poor methods may persist for long periods of time. "Weak sisters" tend to continue in the job—they are not disciplined or weeded out. These conditions are typical when the manager has not recognized that *full accountability for the work of each of his men should be placed with one supervisor.*

The job of a lead man, a senior clerk, or a work director (a worker who also does some supervising of others) usually creates a two-boss setup. On the surface, lead-man operation looks tempting to a manager because he is getting some actual work from the supervisor (the man is not just overhead). However, such an approach tends to deemphasize supervision. Many of the supervisory responsibilities listed in Chapter 8, pages 83 to 87, are not assumed by the lead man—training, holding to account, discipline, etc. The manager must therefore reassume them. However, since he more or less feels that the lead man is supervising the group, he, in turn, tends to let these supervisory responsibilities go by the board. As a consequence, the man on the job is almost always given inadequate supervision.

A lead man in a plant or office will frequently not discipline an employee, call him to account, or take full responsibility for training him, particularly if a union is involved. A senior salesman who is expected to train in a new man may only train him on part of the work. He will often show the new man only the easy accounts in order to impress him. He does not feel fully accountable for the early success of the trainee. A work director in the laboratory may tell a new man what to do. He often fails to follow up, or to assume full responsibility for the well-rounded training or development of the new man. As a consequence, technical men do not develop as fast as had been hoped. All of these lead-man operations have one major weakness. The lead man does not feel personally and fully accountable for the total accomplishment and cost of the subordinate. Without this sense of accountability, you inevitably get loosenesses in the operation and less attention to the man on the job. He therefore does not develop as fast.

There is another way that a double supervisory setup might occur. The manager becomes so busy that he needs an assistant. How does he set the job up? Very often for the assistant to generally "assist" the manager in all his work and to take on "special assignments" (not defined). As likely as not, the two confer on a problem. The assistant goes to a supervisor to give an order; he reports back to the manager on what he told the supervisor. Very likely the manager also goes to the same supervisor and gives other orders or checks up on accomplishment. The result: a two-manager setup. It is unusual if you get more than 50 per cent value out of the assistant. In addition, the setup is very confusing to the individual supervisors. They are not sure which man they should follow. The assistant manager system is quite prevalent in many government departments and in firms that view it as a means by itself for getting back-up for the manager. The latter aim is usually not realized, because men develop best by being held accountable for a result. In this case the assistant manager is only accountable for "assisting."

How should the manager correct the problem? He should give his assistant specific and continued responsibility for some of the results that the manager is trying to achieve, so that the assistant can be held accountable. (Perhaps he should take over complete supervision of some of the supervisors.) The assistant then acquires a sense of accountability for accomplishment as he goes along. He develops more rapidly. The manager has better back-up for his own job.

Some managers feel that they are satisfying the one-boss requirement when they have a man report to one boss on one particular phase of work and report to another on another phase. They say this is a one-boss setup; one boss on each part. This is erroneous thinking. Who is to hold the man uniformly accountable? Who is to decide which part of the work he is to stress at a particular period of time? Who is to discipline the man or take a responsibility for his general training? These and other aspects of supervision will probably go by the board, leading inevitably to poor operation.

Span of Control—Number of People

Every time a supervisor adds a person to his staff, he adds some problems for himself. Each person has his individual idiosyncrasies. Each looks at things differently; each requires different training and special stimulation. *A supervisor can supervise only a limited number of men,* or he exceeds his span of control and cannot carry through on all the elements of supervision. Poor morale, poor employee application, poor scheduling, and low average individual results often occur because a supervisor has exceeded his span of control.

How many men can one supervisor direct? As a rule of thumb, if the work is simple, repetitive, and similar, a typical supervisor is ordinarily able to supervise 25 to 30 people. If he is asked to supervise 40 or 50, it is questionable whether he can carry through on a full supervisory job. The number of people supervised is usually the starting point on deciding optimum span of control: Training problems, problems in clarifying objectives, in disciplining, in holding individual people accountable—all are increased as you add each person to the payroll.

Span of Control—New vs. *Trained Employees*

Even if a manager has determined the correct number of people that a supervisor can handle, he must organize to meet present conditions. A manager is often surprised by the lack of individual accomplishment when his operation expands rapidly and he adds many new employees, or when he sets up a new location. He may fail to recognize the problems that new employees present. *If employees are new or inexperienced, a supervisor cannot effectively supervise as many people.* The problems of training and getting people accustomed to the jobs are multiplied.

For example, a firm that has been going along for some time with essentially the same employees suddenly expands its operation. New employees take an inordinate amount of time to get up to a good level of production. The caliber of the people hired is often blamed. It is more often the fault of the manager in not providing for adequate supervision in this period when so much training and break-in are necessary. The fact that many errors occur, sometimes major ones, and that they are repeated is very often due to inadequate supervision for new employees.

Span of control is frequently overlooked when a firm sets up a new plant or adds additional territories. The new locations do not seem to come up to expectations in the expected time. It takes time for employees to get to understand all the intricacies of the operation, to understand the company, its policies, its objectives, its mode of operation. The supervisor must teach these to each man. If a firm were to hire many new employees from a local area and assign the same number of employees per supervisor as they previously had in an old location, they will almost certainly get costly operation. A workable rule of thumb is to set up twice the previous supervisory force for a period of time. To be sure, after the break-in period, the supervisory force must be cut back or this extra supervision will come to be accepted as normal.

The same problem may occur when a firm is expanding its sales force. Because of the special training problems in learning sales techniques and customer sensitivity, double (or even triple) the supervisory force might be needed immediately to take care of the break-in and training requirements for getting these new men going. This is almost always money well spent. We assume that the supervisors themselves are well trained so that they can effectively train in the new salesmen.

Span of Control—New Functions

A related problem is that of new functions. These may also incur high waste and cost. Sometimes it takes a long time to get new departments up to expectations. New departments add people but do not produce what was expected. Managers either wonder whether they have the right people on these jobs or take this extra break-in cost too much for granted. Violation of span of control may be the cause.

You can readily see (going back to Chapter 8, page 83) that the requirements of supervision in training, in setting objectives, in holding to account, in assigning work, in following up, etc., are multiplied. *When a supervisor is supervising a new or changing function, fewer people must be assigned to him* for the period of time necessary to get the function going well. Little is yet known about the problems presented by the new function. The installation of any procedure generally requires more time than does its maintenance. This is the reason why more supervision is needed when you are trying to break into a new market in sales. The training of people on the missionary work and the new angles involved ordinarily takes more time than usual. More supervision is needed when you wish to develop a new operating department that you did not have before. In an office, a change to more complicated machine operation generally requires increased supervision, because so many of the new procedures and methods will be unfamiliar.

In new operations there is frequently a tendency to augment supervision with staff specialists instead of extra supervisors. This is usually a mistake. What you need in the break-in periods is more supervisors, not more specialists sitting on the side line to further confuse the issue.

As soon as the operation has settled in, it should be

promptly scrutinized for reorganization. Otherwise there is a natural tendency to justify the enlarged supervisory setup as normal. This review of the organization setup should be planned in advance, or it often goes by the board.

Span of Control—Geographical Location

But there are other problems connected with span of control. Ordinarily supervisors are about as effective as their face-to-face relationship. The more they are removed from their people, the more difficult it is to carry out all the elements of supervision mentioned in Chapter 8, pages 83 to 87. Errors tend to continue without correction. Improvements or changes do not take hold, and people are not familiar with company policy or with the implications of objectives. Written orders or explanations do not solve the problem, because people do not seem to catch on as quickly when they rely on written communications. As a consequence *a supervisor cannot supervise as many men when he is physically removed from them.*

As a case in point, a district sales manager cannot effectively direct as many men as an office supervisor. His people are removed from him, so that it is more difficult to maintain adequate face-to-face contact. A district sales manager is therefore most effective when he travels extensively with his men, but this takes time. He can't be with each man as much as can an office supervisor. The value of written communication is extremely limited. It is difficult at best for a man to write even the simplest instructions in such a way that a number of other men will quickly grasp all of the denotations and connotations of the writing. In addition, it is difficult to spur men on to greater effort by a report or a letter. Anyone understands this who has talked to salesmen in regard to the reports and letters that they receive.

A hospital has this problem in building maintenance. It is difficult for the supervisor to supervise well because part of his group is on each of six floors. His crew must be reduced. In doing this it would be good management planning to try to set up responsibilities so that a supervisor has all his people on as few floors as possible.

An executive located in "executive row," away from his subordinates, will find it difficult to coordinate their work. He may get little team spirit among his subordinates. His very location may discourage face-to-face contacts with his men. It is then difficult to make sure that he is stimulating them, that he is developing them, that there is a clear understanding of objectives, etc. Obviously this disadvantage must be balanced against the advantage of being close to decisions in other functions.

There are some special implications to the problem of span of control as it relates to geographical location. In some cases a private office may separate a supervisor from his people, making it more difficult for him to supervise the same number. One cost supervisor who acquired a private office then required an increase of 10 per cent in his crew. He found that, since he was not as close to his people as he had been formerly, he needed more personnel to get out the same amount of work.

A similar problem may face a supervisor who is involved in many meetings. In effect, they separate him geographically from his people. He therefore cannot supervise as many. Executives should give this problem particular attention if they or their subordinates are constantly in meetings. The time they can spend with subordinates in face-to-face contact will be limited—another disadvantage of committees. It must be given weight in designing the management structure.

"Results" Delegation Increases the Span

Ordinarily men operate better if they know exactly what is expected of them—one of the advantages of setting objectives. Direction is pointed out, training is made easier, and accountability becomes more effective. *If a manager and his supervisors have each delegated by objectives, the number of people they can supervise is increased.* Records can be developed so that accomplishment speaks for itself. It is then much easier to operate confidently with a flattened-out organization structure, because final accountability has been effectively set up.

Of course, standards or objectives must be carefully thought out as they relate to the work of other supervisors and other men so that there is a minimum of interference of one man with another. The number of interrelationships that the manager must smooth over will be decreased and his span of control therefore increased.

A Manager Must Not Bypass a Supervisor

Sometimes a manager becomes concerned because his supervisors do not appear to take responsibility. They are always calling on the manager instead of solving their own problems. Different methods are used for the same kind of work; he feels that they ought to be made more uniform, so he straightens them out. Perhaps the supervisors take the attitude that their job is that of being available to their men for help rather than of aggressively supervising to make sure that a good job is well done. Although the tendency is to blame the supervisors, these situations often occur because of the way the manager himself operates. In effect, he may not have completed his delegation. He may have failed to recognize the amount of authority that goes with the delegation of a responsibility.

Perhaps the manager goes around a supervisor and discusses problems directly with the man. He may do this because he feels he should be in touch or that he should be a stimulant. He does not realize, however, the implications of his comments for the man down the line. In effect, any comment of his is likely to be viewed as an order. He may see some problem occurring and go directly to the man on the job to ask about it. The man, of course, immediately straightens out the problem. When the man's own supervisor asks him about it, his natural comment is, "The manager said I should do this." The action has retracted part of the manager's delegation to the supervisor. The supervisor will not feel as accountable for the results that have been laid out for him, because the manager has actually pulled back part of his delegation. The men down the line tend to look at their supervisors with less respect, making it more difficult for the supervisors to hold their men accountable.

The manager should not give orders directly to the men under his supervisors. If he does, he will, in effect, weaken his delegation. A manager may feel that he simply made a suggestion that would help the operation. However, he must visualize the effect on the man down the line. In case of grave emergency, of course, a manager may give an order to the man, but he should immediately notify the supervisor or leave a note so that the supervisor may then take appropriate action, either to continue with the order or to change it. There should be a clear understanding that the supervisor has this authority.

A supervisor who has been promoted to the position of a manager must be especially watchful to avoid this inclination. He should be coached on it by his superior. The problem must be guarded against at every level straight through to that of president. A manager can no longer operate directly the way he did as a supervisor, even on those problems that he knows very well. A foreman who has been made a superintendent cannot go back to his old department and tell the individual operators how to do their jobs. A district manager who is promoted to regional or general sales manager must be very careful that he is not available to the individual salesmen for solving their problems. (Of course, a president who came up through the sales field must exercise the same personal discipline.) The "open door" policy has frequently been misunderstood and has actually led to a vitiation of the delegation from a manager to his supervisors. It can seriously impair the supervisory-subordinate relationship of the supervisors.

10

Encourage Supervisory Decision Making

As a manager becomes more removed from first-line problems, he is frequently appalled by the errors and lack of accomplishment down the line. It appears to him that his supervisors do not act as he did. They do not seem to make the kinds of decisions that he did and they do not make them promptly. They revere the *status quo,* and new methods and new approaches are very rarely attempted. He cannot understand why his supervisors do not step out and take more aggressive action. It is difficult for him to be introspective and recognize that these problems may lie with him. As his responsibility has broadened, his concept of the errors to be allowed down below may not have broadened with it. In effect, the manager is not allowing his supervisors the leeway that he enjoyed when he was in their position. As a consequence, they in turn cannot make decisions as he did and they do not grow the way they should. New programs are not assimilated, and incisive action is not taken.

Broaden a Supervisor's Authority

A supervisor cannot take incisive action nor can he, in turn, delegate the freedom to make errors to his own people unless the manager has first given the supervisor fairly broad authority. The manager can easily lose sight of this necessity. It is natural for a manager to be careful about giving authority. The usual rationalization is, "They have to learn to use authority effectively first." He forgets the number of errors he made on similar jobs, and that his total accomplishment was much greater because he had this leeway. If an operation is to be effective, *each level in the organization echelon should have broader authority than the level below.*

A manager must acquire a new perspective; he must now permit a supervisor to make errors that are greater than he permitted his subordinates to make when he was a supervisor. His approach to authority should be much the same as it was when he was a supervisor. He should first determine the objectives that the supervisor is expected to accomplish. After this he should determine the breadth of decision and the probable errors that might be expected of the supervisor if he were aggressive in pursuing his objectives. A difficult transition in thinking is required of a man climbing up the management chain.

An office supervisor who is made office manager quite

naturally has difficulty allowing his supervisors to discipline their people and determine methods. He somehow feels that he alone has a natural touch; he cannot quite believe that they can handle these difficult problems, forgetting that he handled them when he was a supervisor. He therefore tends to constrict their allowance for errors below what he himself formerly enjoyed, and his supervisors do not develop to handle their own problems. This proves to his satisfaction that he was right in the first place in not permitting them to make some of these decisions and he tends to retain even more authority for himself.

The same problem may exist in an over-the-road trucking company with a terminal manager who controls all operations in his district. When he held this position, he fully recognized how important this control was to his effectiveness as a terminal manager. When he is promoted to the position of operations manager, however, he is inclined to remember the consummate skill with which he made these decisions. He therefore feels that he can make decisions more effectively for all the districts by setting up fixed policies and procedures requiring many of the decisions to come up to him. He forgets that when he was a terminal manager it was imperative that he make such decisions on the spot in the light of changing conditions. He was then, however, much closer to the problems.

Failure to redelegate authority is one of the greatest weaknesses of large, growing organizations—as a man goes up each echelon his delegation of authority does not broaden with the scope of his responsibility. As a consequence, men do not grow at all levels through being able to exercise authority. Instead, paper work multiplies, presumably to keep people at the higher levels informed, and exercises an even stronger influence toward centralization of decisions.

You can readily see that policies must become broader the higher a man goes. At every level the leeway to make decisions must be greater than it was at one level below. Otherwise, every change has to come up to the manager. This has strong implications in large firms for the authority that must be delegated from a general manager to his vice-presidents. If this delegation is not broad enough, decision making at the bottom levels is inevitably strapped. There is not enough authority at the vice-presidential level to subdivide all the way down. Method changes will not be permitted without consultation; the manager has to be in on every employee problem; almost every requisition must be approved by someone above. Under these conditions it is difficult to develop supervisors and the firm seems to have a dearth of promotable material. The firm actually has, however, all the ability that it needs—lying dormant.

Push Decisions to the Lowest Level

In the very elementary stage of organization where one man works for another, each develops a respect for the ability of the other. Each understands the problems of the other. As the firm grows larger and more complex, however, there is a tendency for a countertrend to develop. A manager may have trouble developing respect for his supervisors. They just do not seem to him to be capable. He therefore feels that he must make all the decisions himself. It appears, to him at least, that decisions are not made when they are needed and are not always sound. Decision making generally tends to climb upward to him, the only place where, in his estimation, any real competency exists. This centralization will tend to occur quite naturally if a manager has not decided to *force the decisions to the lowest level possible.* Decisions tied into the objectives expected of a supervisor should be made by that supervisor unless they seriously impinge on the work of other supervisors. Only the exceptional decision of broad importance should come up to the manager. Otherwise, it is difficult to encourage the supervisor in turn to delegate decision making to his subordinates.

In many plants a foreman should go as far as possible in making current decisions on waste, on employee control, and on scheduling for his machines, because these are explicitly tied into the cost of producing in his department. It is only when these decisions have major implications for other departments, or when the dollar effect of a "normal" decision is so great that the superintendent or plant manager could not allow a foreman to make it, that it should come up to him.

There is a natural tendency for a manager to retain all decision making when a decision on part of a problem requires his approval. It seems clear to him that he must therefore make the decisions on all parts of the problem. Any function may at times require decisions of major importance. This does not mean, however, that the secondary problems connected with that function cannot be solved, and probably solved better, by the individual supervisor of the function. It is important that the manager carefully scrutinize the whole situation to make sure that all parts of a major problem that can be solved by a subordinate are delegated to the subordinate. This is fundamental for the development of an aggressive, responsible force down the line.

A general sales manager may feel that the question of sales planning is of major importance in the results he should achieve for his firm. He may be right, but this does not mean that certain elements in the planning of approaches to individual territories or customers would not be better made, within limits, by individual district sales managers, or by salesmen if they can be held accountable. Strong company-mindedness will then develop in the sales force all the way down the line.

The same problem exists in an office. It may be true that a chief accountant must make sure that certain standards and tie-ins are maintained. Many decisions on methods, preparation of reports, and their interpretation may be made by accounting supervisors, however, if accountability has been established. The supervisors then become much broader, more capable of future promotion.

STIMULATE SUPERVISORS WITH RECORDS

One of the problems that plague any manager is a tendency for supervisors to be satisfied with below-par performance. Supervisors may feel that their work must be all right because nothing serious has happened. Therefore they do not push improvement nor are they quick to weed out the little inefficiencies that always tend to creep into an operation. Poor trends in accomplishment or cost are not assumed as their personal responsibility. The attitude can stem from the fact that little information is given to the supervisor. He may not be aware of the importance of problems in his group. The record approach that applies to individuals, pointed up in Chapter 8, page 80, also should apply to supervisors: The record system should be tied specifically to each supervisor's results; he should be notified of deviations.

A Supervisor Should Be Informed

Many accounting records are not broken down so that supervisors can be informed. For example, cost records are frequently not developed by individual operations. As a consequence, the supervisor will not be aware of the places where his employees are deviating. In addition, records by type of operation, by section, by significant variation in period, are not presented. It is, therefore, extremely difficult for the supervisor, first, to be actively aware that these are his problems, and secondly, to know just exactly where the problems are and their significance. He may therefore focus on the wrong areas; he may not take strong steps to straighten out weak employees; finally, he may simply rely on general meetings in the hope of straightening out weak spots in his operation. *The supervisor should know the trend of accomplishment of each man in specific short-term periods.* He must know when the deviations are beyond the limits of decision that he wished the man to observe. The accumulation of this data helps him set objectives.

District sales managers frequently do not get enough information on their accomplishment by product, by fluctuation, by profit, and perhaps even by individual types of accounts. Much of this information would be most effective if it were given directly to the salesman on a current basis. In many firms such a procedure is rarely even considered. As a consequence the salesman does not really know where he is deviating from sound company accomplishment. There are added implications when a salesman is promoted to district sales manager. He has difficulty in using what information is given him and in putting it into its perspective.

The Supervisor Gets the First Chance

As a firm grows, upper management desires more and more information, so record systems become highlighted. Supervisors often resent these records. They dislike wasting their time, as they put it, to provide information for "unnecessary" reports. They dislike the idea of being shown up by the records. When some record is discussed with them, they may alibi instead of attempting to correct the problem. As a consequence, the firm may get very limited value from its excellent records except by constant pressure. Many firms accept this situation as a natural consequence of keeping records. It need not be so.

The person who is running the record system should *report deviations to the supervisor first,* before he reports them to the manager. In other words, if an objective has been defined for a supervisor and he is deviating from it, he should be informed of this deviation (if it is within his authority) so that he has a chance to take corrective action. (If it is within the authority of the man below him, it should not even come to the supervisor.) It is only when these deviations have exceeded the supervisor's authority that his manager should be informed of them. Such a record procedure is difficult for a manager to accept. In effect, he must design the responsibility of the record people in such a way that they do **not** report these minor deviations to him, but only to the supervisor.

Note what happens if this information comes to the manager. It would take a manager of almost superhuman discipline to keep from observing and asking pointed questions on any deviation shown in the reports. The effect on a supervisor is to put him on the defensive. He feels that he should not have made the deviation. He becomes very careful, first, about making any decisions that may show up as deviations and secondly, about the way he reports information so that deviations will not show up on the reports. His whole concept of his own authority may be subtly undermined. Many managers decry this tendency, failing to realize that it is a normal one for any supervisor under these conditions.

When the information is reported to the supervisor instead of to the manager, the record system assists each individual supervisor to broaden his perspective and to take constructive action on problems. It forces home an appreciation of his responsibility. The exception principle is highlighted, and the supervisor is encouraged to develop his own judgment and ingenuity.

Effect of a Cost Reduction Program

Problems with record systems are multiplied during a cost reduction period. It is natural for a manager to want to get tight control of every item at that time. What happens? The supervisor feels that he doesn't dare move because a minor cost may show up in the records and point out that he is not "cooperating" with the cost program. He therefore waits for pressure. He does not take any strong action until he gets pressure in a particular direction. He may know the right way to move, but he sits tight. He is not sure how the move may show up on the reports. He tends to hold to the *status quo* until he gets specific orders—usually the safest thing to do as he is then relieved of accountability. In desperation the manager issues a blanket order of an *x* per cent cut in cost across the board in order to get action.

Record systems developed in cost reduction periods may have an adverse effect for five or ten years afterward, an effect that may not even be realized, but traceable to a poor design of the organization setup for the record system. Record people have not been made firmly accountable for tying their records in with the total responsibility of the individual supervisor. They may merely suggest blanket cuts in expenditures, probably in expenditures on indirect help. The adverse effect of these cuts on operations may not be noticed until several years afterward. One of the big advantages of setting management objectives is that the method of operating under this procedure is no different in tight periods than it is in other periods. In a cost reduction period, objectives may simply be different, but the same drive is demanded in all periods. There is more constancy to the operation and the panic effect of a tight business period is reduced. Employees feel more secure.

As the firm grows more complex, an essential part of the delegation of the manager is a setup for the responsibility and the mode of operation of his record people. He must develop insight and managerial perspective in the record men, as they can have far-reaching effects on the development of insight and managerial perspective in all his supervisors. The record system can decidedly aid or retard the growth of a vigorous, responsible management team.

11

Complexity of Supervising Variable Positions

WHAT ARE the differences when the work of a supervisor requires that he delegate to a number of people, each doing different kinds of work even though they are all in one group or section? Setting objectives is more time-consuming. The supervisor must also develop training methods on a variety of work—this takes more time. A broader understanding is required of the integration of different kinds of work. People are more easily confused as to what is expected of them, and some tasks do not get done. Narrow specialists may develop who disregard their relationships with others. In general, a new dimension seems to enter the management picture, requiring more insight and better coordination if sound accomplishment is to be obtained from all employees.

Aim Toward the Average Person

Supervisors wish to get the very best men available. There is a natural tendency, therefore, to design jobs so that the hiring requirement is extraordinarily high. The argument given is, "We don't want any average person," under the supposition that setting up a high requirement for hiring will assure outstanding accomplishment. The firm very often finds, however, that it does not have good men to promote, and that much of the work does not come up to what it would expect, primarily because very selective hiring is extremely difficult. In addition, much of the success on a job does not depend so much on hiring as it does on the management climate and on the training and development of the individual. It is therefore a much better practice for a supervisor to *define each job as far as possible so that the average person employed for the job could do it satisfactorily.*

Good organization design strives toward a setup in which the average person employed could do the job reasonably well, but with ample opportunity for the unusual person to achieve much greater accomplishment. In other words, you are designing with fences on the side but with unlimited opportunity ahead. Most jobs lend themselves to such a design. Such a setup provides for guided development of the individual on the job without excessive pressure.

Apply the Principle of Specialization

It is perfectly normal for a supervisor to want to have flexibility. It appears logical to train all his people on all the work of his unit. When the work is variable, however, the employees may develop to be jacks-of-all-trades and masters of none. Jobs never seem to get completely done. Perhaps the firm is unable to utilize new scientific developments and new methods. The very methods may require a considerable amount of time to understand. If everyone is to understand all methods, the best each person can do is to acquire a superficial understanding.

There is a limit as to how much one man can know and know well. In addition, every time a man must have additional knowledge, extra training is required. Demanding more than one special ability or skill may make the hiring requirements too difficult. It is hard for a supervisor to get full accomplishment from the job.

Delegate by specialization, if at all possible. In setting up a job, require no more than one specialized ability or background. Wherever a job requires several, you should consider changing the setup of the job. In some cases, of course, this is impossible. It is a good rule to keep in mind, however, so that complexity in job requirements is minimized.

For example, a job may require high intelligence. At the same time a high level of a second ability may also be required—the ability to influence people. The difficulty is that the two abilities do not necessarily occur together. In other words, it is unlikely that you will find the same people outstanding in the second ability as were outstanding in the first. At the present stage of development of interviewing and placement techniques, finding the two qualities in one person may be almost an impossible hiring requirement for the supervisor. He has designed the job for failure!

The problem is typical when a firm makes up a long list of requirements or traits required to fill a job. Such a procedure seems perfectly logical on the surface; it smacks of the scientific approach—suggesting that someone has carefully analyzed the job. However, if all the requirements listed, such as ingenuity, judgment, intelligence, mechanical ability, contact ability, etc., were taken seriously, there is probably no one individual who could possibly completely qualify for the position.

Sales supervisors of technical or semitechnical firms very often have difficulty reconciling hiring requirements. It appears that a sales engineer's job requires a high degree of mechanical ability. At the same time, the manager feels the man should be good at making contacts. It may be quite hard to find both abilities in the same man. In many cases a person who has average mechanical ability, coupled with very good contact ability, will do a good job. The latter may be the key requirement for success. If this basic requirement is not recognized, the manager is quite likely to compromise on the contact ability in favor of high mechanical ability and actually get inferior results. Poor management design has led the manager to poor operation.

We are really saying that the supervisor should carefully analyze the job to determine the critical ability requirement that makes or breaks the accomplishment. He should try to hire someone with this critical requirement even though some other apparently valuable requirements may go by the board. The supervisor will usually get more effective administration without having to worry about many minor requirements when hiring. Subordinate positions are put in better perspective. The supervisor will see more clearly where and how he may apply the rule of errors—what activities may go wrong without seriously affecting the major accomplishment expected of the position.

Be Careful of Overspecialization

There is a counterproblem occurring with many supervisors, that of overspecialization. Because of the influence of Taylor and industrial engineering principles, many people believe that the most effective way to design jobs is to break down all work so that each position involves only a simplified element of activity. An efficiency-minded manager might be inclined to do this in an office, a plant, or a sales department. It seems logical: because less training is required, a person should be able to acquire a reasonable proficiency in a simplified task in a hurry. Specialization may be overdone, however. Parts of the work may become so disjointed that many committee meetings develop in order to "coordinate." Constant daily or weekly meetings are needed to meet current problems.

Offices often experience a great increase in payroll but get less output per person. It may occur this way. As a company grows each person is assigned minute breakdowns of activity. The number of times each piece of paper is handled increases. In addition, little empires prosper and grow in groups of these activities, intensifying the problem of coordination. It is only natural for people to become insular and less aware of the related problems of others.

Very frequently expensive equipment installations are

justified under these conditions because, in effect, they will reverse this trend. Good management planning might very well have done just as well and at less cost. One of the main advantages of the equipment installation was merely that it recombined tasks by final result. The basic rule holds: *even though you specialize, avoid breaking down accountability for a result* as much as possible. Ask yourself this question, "What is this job supposed to accomplish?" Then try to combine as much of the work necessary to the accomplishment of that result as you can.

Overspecialization becomes intensified because of the degree of specialization that has occurred in our society. Specialized groups seem to have a natural desire to develop a "professionalized attitude." Tied to this, of course, is the desire to increase the stature of their positions. They tend to overweigh "the requirements of the profession." They give more attention to the code of ethics or "standard procedures" of their specialties than to accomplishment. They may emphasize activities rather than what the job should do for the firm and demand status because of their position or knowledge, rather than status as a result of their accomplishment.

A skilled man may overemphasize the quality of his work (as he sees it) and so get less output. Skilled office employees or technical men may easily do this. A statistician or economist may glow over the neatness and voluminousness of his reports but become unconcerned about the actual use of these reports. In a police department a traffic officer may be proud of the number of traffic tickets issued but feel little personal accountability for the number of accidents occurring or for the restrictions on personal freedom he may impose.

It is easy for a supervisor or executive to succumb to the pressure of these groups. He is usually well advised, however, to disregard the "normal" specialized groups when organizing. The specialized breakdown very rarely fits the results demanded in a particular firm. More often than not it leads to a greatly overstaffed organization with unsatisfactory accomplishment. Carrying specialization too far also leaves gaps in results with no one assuming responsibility. Delegating by total results, even though it oversteps some specialties, tends to prevent this.

BLEND MANAGEMENT RESULTS

Although total accomplishment is made up of many individual accomplishments of individual men, in a broad sense a manager must view all results as group results. All the individual accomplishments must be blended in some way so that they mesh. He must keep all individuals headed in the same over-all direction. One individual may wish to star—to outshine others and thereby go in a counterdirection. The over-all accomplishment may lag because of a lag in a result on which others depend, and bottlenecks may occur. One of the most critical and searching questions that a manager must ask is, "What is the best way to blend the results of all my people?" The question takes on additional nuances when the individuals are doing different kinds of work.

What Is the Value of the Result?

When people are working on a variety of jobs, changing emphasis is often needed. Some of the accomplishments may be more important than others in one period of time in order to realize over-all goals. Many minor items may be pushed, with an illusion of commendable achievement, while major accomplishments are not made. Men normally avoid the more difficult problems, secure in the feeling that many of the minor items are accomplished. In dealing with a variety of work, as opposed to one kind, it is more difficult to retain perspective. As a consequence, a supervisor may have an interested crew, a great deal of work being done, and perhaps high morale, but low over-all accomplishment, considering what he expected.

As we stated in Chapter 2, page 10, in laying out the results expected, care must be taken to point out which results are primary and which are secondary. When the employees are doing a variety of work, extra care is required, since it is difficult to evaluate the relative value of the results. If this evaluation is not made, the employee cannot feel the accountability that is necessary. As a consequence worthwhile achievement is reduced.

Because of some past difficulties in the plant, a superintendent may have stressed with his foremen good housekeeping, good record keeping, and good maintenance. These, of course, are all part of the job. However, because of this emphasis, control of the cost of production, waste, and perhaps quality of goods produced may not have been emphasized and may therefore have lagged. It would be only natural for his foremen to focus on the areas emphasized by the superintendent.

A design engineering supervisor may have emphasized the number of tests and analyses completed. The very number and variety of these seem to give them importance.

Naturally each of his engineers feels that if he carries out many tests and analyses, he has done a good job. But he may have missed two major requirements: first, that they lead to a product that is salable, and secondly, that they lead to a product that is producible at a reasonable cost in the company's plant. If he is to emphasize these last two requirements, it is imperative that the supervisor clearly state that they are major requirements of the job. It is true, of course, that various tests, analyses, and experiments may be viewed as guideposts along the way and make their contributions. But this should never obscure the fact that the real accomplishment is the final result of all these actions and the way that the result helps the firm.

Should You Organize around the Man?

Some supervisors say they like to define the organization "around people." By this they usually mean that they would like to give a strong man all the difficult tasks that he can possibly handle. The philosophy sounds very logical, but it almost always leads to poor management design.

Suppose a supervisor is in charge of four men and delegates responsibility for results to each. One of these is an outstanding employee (*A* in Figure 8). He is the kind we would all like to have! The other three (*B*, *C*, and *D*) are weak. If a difficult project develops in the area of one of the weak employees (*B*), it is natural for the supervisor to ask the strong man to do it (he feels he can rely on the star performer). In effect, this pulls away part of the original delegation to the weak employee. It relieves him of full accountability for the total results assigned to him.

If another difficult project occurs in the area of another weak employee (*C* or *D*), the supervisor is inclined to also give it to the strong man. He may do this repeatedly in any of the areas of the weak people. What is the consequence?

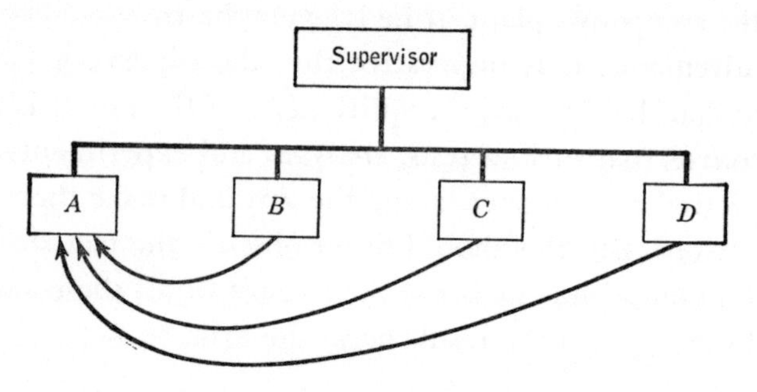

FIG. 8 Imbalance in delegation.

Since the strong man is carrying most of the important work of the department, he becomes so overburdened that he has to let some of his work go. He feels perfectly justified in doing this. He simply has too much to do. As a consequence the good man develops sloppy habits of accountability which, in effect, weaken him. (In addition, he may become so overworked that he gets a heart attack.)

But what happens to the weak employees? They become weaker. Since they have been relieved of the difficult part of their work, they feel less accountable for total results. They do not develop a sense of accountability for results delegated to them. The supervisor's department has deteriorated rather than grown stronger. The weakness becomes apparent should the strong man leave. Then the supervisor has increased difficulty getting the work done. His department is out of balance.

Such a supervisor would have been well advised to insist on accomplishment of all results assigned to his men. Part of the supervisory job should be that of developing each man up to the point where he can get reasonable accomplishment of all his assigned results. It is one of his obligations. The supervisor who does not do this will find that he has a weaker department. On the other hand, if he does follow through and build up these men to at least reasonable performance, over a period of time he will get a much greater total accomplishment from all his people with considerably less trouble.

Give Subordinates Equal Responsibility

A supervisor may delegate the bulk of his major results to one man and divide the minor ones among the rest of his people. The supervisor is not using his own time well in that case. He becomes overburdened by the task of supervising minor activities. *A supervisor should delegate equal responsibility to each of his subordinates* if at all possible—normally better than having one subordinate carry a much heavier responsibility than is required of the others. It prevents any one person from being excessively critical to the total accomplishment. The supervisor will find that he has a better control of his operation and is more flexible to meet varying conditions as they arise.

One way to do this is for the supervisor to list all the results to be accomplished by his group. Then select the most critical results and, if possible, delegate at least one of these important results to each subordinate. If he finds that a subordinate has none of these, he should reconsider his delegation so that every man is set up to achieve at least one important part of the total accomplishment. By this approach the supervisor is forced to carefully consider his delegations to be sure that they are in balance. It is easier, then, to keep on top of all the key areas.

DEVELOP A DESIGN FOR COOPERATION

We said earlier that in the final analysis most results in a company tend to be cooperative results. They depend on a blending of the work of a number of people. It is especially important that these cooperative aspects be thoroughly thought out when the work is diversified, especially those that tie in closely with each other. It is easy for head-on collisions to develop, so that instead of cooperating each person goes on his own merry way with much less total accomplishment, often retarding the work of another.

Do Not Rely on Contrary Interest

It is natural for supervisors to feel that all employees should be loyal and willing to help each other. They often forget, however, that the setting of the job may militate against this. Perhaps a man depends on the help of another who really has entirely antagonistic objectives. Parts of a job may lag and troubles will be constantly occurring between two men—often the reason why skilled men don't carry through. *No one should be dependent on the activity of another person of contrary interest.*

Very often the results expected of the person of contrary interest can be revised to make them compatible with those of his coworker. In other words, redesign his job so that the interests of the two will blend rather than be contrary. Not only is the conflict reduced but also the requirement for coordinating on the part of the supervisor. A supervisor who does not take the time to work this out will find himself spending an inordinate amount of time supervising and mediating, usually with less result.

A typical example occurs in a plant. Perhaps an operator is on a bonus plan with no deductions made for poor quality. Poor quality, however, may be a severe handicap to subsequent operations. Under these conditions it is only natural that the operator would give less attention to quality and primary consideration to quantity. In effect, the results of the job of the first operator are antagonistic to the achievement of good results by subsequent operators. Trouble naturally develops and quite a bit of discussion is needed to iron out the problems. The basic setting encourages these problems.

A similar situation could occur in the laboratory. A research engineer may feel that a product should be developed in a particular way. To him this will make a "good product." Although the product will be difficult to sell the way he designs it, he is inclined to fight any suggestion of a change in his design. If, however, he is made accountable in some way for the sales realized in the first years of production of the product, he is much more apt to be in harmony with the sales department. He is more inclined to ask their advice and to carefully work out a product that "sells."

It is only natural for sales managers to push volume and

worry little about schedules, close timing problems, and special demands made on the plant. Perhaps the problem of variability in ups and downs in sales is brushed off quickly with the comment, "This is the way the customer buys." The comment may be true and with the emphasis on volume it is perfectly natural for the sales group to take this attitude. It is, however, strongly antagonistic to sound, efficient results in the plant. The chief executive should carefully consider necessary tie-in results between his sales and his production departments so that it is to the advantage of the sales department to work toward efficient production without affecting volume unduly.

Design for Harmonious Results

Jealousies and a considerable amount of in-fighting will occur when people have antagonistic objectives. The reluctance to cooperate and perhaps the tendency to blame others may also be traceable to this. A supervisor should try to *make all results expected of each man harmonious with those expected of other men.* He should make this his active rather than his passive responsibility.

For example, constant problems may occur between scheduling and operating people. The schedulers want to line up the work so that they get products out on time, though their schedule may lead to inefficient runs, to difficulties in dovetailing work in crews, and to union problems. There may also be excessive stockpiling of goods in process. The schedulers may not feel accountable for these operating difficulties. It is much more effective to make them accountable in some way for the final consequence, whether it be cost, waste, or excessive crew. It is then to their interest to give more consideration to operating problems. The design of the results expected of a man should make it to his advantage to give needed help to others.

A similar problem could occur in a bank. Customers of one man may be prospects for men in other departments. However, unless these cooperative results are made part of the responsibility of the first man, he will not always refer the customer to his coworkers. Admonishing him to be a "company man" does not usually accomplish this, especially if the man is evaluated only by the accomplishment on his own job. In some way he must get credit for achievement in the other area.

A Man Gets Results

Because the work of any enterprise is really the joint result of all the people in it, there is a natural tendency on the part of a supervisor to look to the group for accomplishment. In most cases a man accomplishes a result. When several people are involved, as they very frequently are, each individual must still be relied on to accomplish a personal share of the total, a distinction that is well worth keeping in mind. Otherwise there is a tendency for "everybody" to be in on everything and for no one to shoulder responsibility. Committee meetings develop, and it seems difficult to fix the blame when anything goes wrong. Corrective action is not taken as soon as it should be. At the same time, men do not become strong, responsible employees. When there is a variety of work to be done, these problems become intensified. There is then a much greater tendency to hold the group rather than the individual accountable, because several people contribute to a result.

The management design should be carefully reviewed so that *a man, not a group, should be accountable for the actual accomplishment of individual results.* As we have indicated before, this accountability is much more effective and meaningful to the employee if it is carried through into appraisals, pay, or any other means of rewarding an employee. To the extent that an employee has an "out" through blaming others or through group meetings, accountability is weakened. To the extent that it is weakened, the employee himself is weakened and does not develop the same sense of self-reliance in meeting problems.

It is quite natural that meetings evolve in any firm as a means of solving problems. Sometimes these develop under the heading of communication. At other times they are coordinating meetings. Very frequently they are postmortem meetings on deviations. But the deviations are always recurring. If these meetings occur often, their frequency should be a signal to the executive that the individual sense of accountability has not been developed. The management design should be reviewed—not the employees.

A related problem occurs in written communications. Whenever a flood of written communications or reports begin to develop to "inform" everybody about conditions, you can be sure that the employees do not have a strong sense of personal accountability—another indication of faulty management design. Very frequently many reports circulate through a company because notifying others of your problems has become a successful way of avoiding accountability. It has been our experience that changing from group (or no) accountability to personal accountability almost automatically cuts down this paper work.

One of the best examples of this problem is a cost committee. A supervisor may be concerned about the adverse trend in costs. It seems sound, therefore, to set up a cost committee of various responsible people to work on the problem in order to give it emphasis. Unfortunately, the creation of such a committee generally leads to less personal accountability. After this group has operated for a while it becomes difficult to get things done without the committee. The individual tends to assume less personal responsibility for cost reduction as a steady requirement of his job. The most regrettable consequence is that over a period of time you may discover that you do not have enough decisive people available for promotion. The cost committee procedure may have weakened the natural initiative of the men in the firm.

Can Committees Help?

You may question, then, whether committees are of any value at all. (For the purposes of this discussion, a committee is any meeting of two or more people to discuss a problem, whether they meet formally or not.) There are places where committees are helpful if properly designed and followed out.

When a group of men get together to discuss a problem, the chairmanship naturally tends to gravitate toward the senior man, the man at the top of the echelon. Strangely enough, he is usually the last person who should be chairman. He tends to relieve others of personal accountability. However, it is quite easy for a supervisor or an executive to slip into this practice. His people just naturally defer to him.

Why is the chairmanship important? One of the basic reasons why committees fail to operate well may be that no one (or else the wrong person) assumes responsibility for its operations and its results. No one person is expected to carry out the committee decisions, to plan ahead, or to follow up to be sure something is accomplished as a result of a meeting. Without a setup for this any committee tends to operate like a rudderless ship.

One of the best ways to correct the problem is to select as chairman the man whose personal job responsibility is most in line with the responsibility of the committee. For example, if the problem to be discussed is one of costs, the cost man should be chairman. If it is an advertising problem, the advertising man should be chairman. Since the chairman is responsible for the results, he should be responsible for preparing an agenda. It should be axiomatic that meetings should not be called unless somebody has thought through an agenda, at least mentally. It should be the job of the chairman to call the meetings, making sure he includes only those people who can assist on the problem under consideration. In too many firms it is a common practice to call everybody to the meeting who might possibly have any interest in it, wasting the time of many people and lengthening committee meetings. It should also be the job of the chairman to run the meeting and make sure that solutions are arrived at and worked out.

Then to the key point: *The chairman has the responsibility to get action* (not the committee members) on the decisions of the committee. You can readily see that he would be interested in doing this because he is responsible for the item under consideration whether you have the committee or not.

What is the responsibility of a member? Ordinarily, the member should be expected to come to the meetings when they are called. He should be expected to contribute ideas along the track suggested by the chairman, particularly ideas in regard to his own function. If action is demanded that is within his own personal responsibility, he should be expected to carry it out at the request of the chairman. With good management design this would be natural because such action is probably tied to his normal responsibility anyway. With this kind of setup you ordinarily get a great deal more out of committees than you otherwise might, and do not require nearly as many committee meetings.

Just a few additional points in regard to committees: If any information is required for committee deliberations, the investigation of these data should be made in advance —the responsibility, of course, of the chairman. Otherwise long periods of time may be spent trying to solve problems for which the necessary facts have not been investigated. There is also a normal inclination of committees to waste time on minor items. With a well-built agenda and a firmly fixed responsibility for the chairman, this weakness can usually be minimized. It is an added help, however, to insist that objectives be set for each item to be considered. In other words, before any problem is even taken up by a committee, the objective of the discussion should be clearly stated. Such direction helps a great deal in keeping everybody on the same wave length.

As we mentioned earlier, it is natural for the top man in the echelon to take over a committee, whether he is chairman or not. To prevent this happening it is helpful if members of the committee are chosen from the same level in the echelon. When there is considerable variation in levels between the men in a committee, it is natural for the people down the line to defer to the men of the highest level. First, they have high regard for the people up the line; secondly, these are the men they look to for future promotion. They are therefore not going to be too adamant in posing objections. As a consequence the committee meeting may not have as good a result, particularly on a sticky problem, as is likely if all its members function on a basis of equality.

12

Encouraging Uniform Results from Variable Positions

Supervising a group of variable positions, as discussed in Chapter 11, often creates difficulties in developing uniform high accomplishment while still maintaining proper direction. There is a tendency for part of the work to go ahead while other parts lag. It seems difficult to keep tag ends from developing. Because there are so many different things to be done, there is a tendency for people to wait for suggestions instead of exhibiting personal initiative. These difficulties frequently arise because the supervisor does not recognize the need for variable accountability or see that broader freedom must be allowed in order to maintain the drive he may have attained when all the work was similar.

FIRM UP ACCOUNTABILITY

When people are doing different kinds of work, it is much more difficult for the supervisor to set objectives and establish sound accountability. This phase of his job becomes more complex. Because each kind of work is different, bottlenecks occur in coordinating one kind with another. It is now difficult to answer the question, "How can this position make the best over-all contribution?" Therefore, important results are not accomplished and the difficult or "dirty" jobs seem to go by the board. An unbalanced operation develops, and the supervisor is constantly faced with trouble. Individual personal accountability must be highlighted so that the work of one person is effectively tied in with that of another. *Each individual must be accountable for meeting tie-in requirements with other positions.*

An example of this necessity occurs in a plant where efficiency is stressed. The timing of the work of one man may seriously affect the output of another. With the emphasis on efficiency, however, it is normal that he would give little consideration to this tie-in requirement. Instead, he may try to get long production runs which may throw off his timing with the needs of the second man. Unless the first man is held firmly accountable for this timing, you may easily get squabbles between the two men. Frequently standards are loosened up to take account of idle time caused by poor timing in the first job or special time allowances are given to the second man. This solution is usually an indication that personal accountability for tie-in performance has not been adequately thought out. The same problem can, of course, occur between two foremen when the quality of the output of the department of one seriously affects the operation of the second department.

In a good restaurant the work of bus boys must be well tied in with that of the waiters both as to timing and to service to the customer. The tie-in is often well met by a setup in which each waiter gives his bus boy a percentage of his tips. The bus boy is then accountable for giving top service to each customer and for handling customers fast. In this way he will help to maximize tips.

Accountability for Results—Not Abortive Action

When a supervisor lets it be known that he expects to hold people accountable, their first reaction is often to exhibit a great deal of hard work, carried out with considerable hustle-bustle and activity. When his people are engaged in variable work, it is especially difficult for a supervisor to differentiate between this activity and concrete results. It is important, therefore, that he think through as to what results should be expected of each man so that he can hold him soundly accountable for accomplishment instead of activity.

The emphasis on results has implications in obtaining improvement all the way through the operation. The requirement for new-methods improvement should be tied to each type of work so that all the operations go ahead. When there are many different types of work, this is hard to do because it is difficult to define the end result toward which the different parts are aiming. Ingenuity is required in designing combinations of work so that men may be held soundly accountable for improvement.

Avoid Divided Accountability

When men work together on a difficult problem, it is frequently hard to maintain their firmness of resolve in facing difficulties that occur. A divided sense of accountability may aggravate this problem. Even though an individual may have to carry out a specified part of the work, the net effect of this part can only be seen in a total result contributed by several individuals. If he is only measured by his part, the gaps between his part and another are never assumed by anyone. *Accountability should be in terms of a measurable result even though others contribute to it.* Further division merely leads to accountability by activity.

This problem shows up in new product development. Perhaps the sales department should develop the initial idea. Then the idea should be market-tested. Then, perhaps, a design should be developed in a preliminary way, based on the engineering information available from market research. This preliminary design should be tested further to see whether the product is practical. The product must then be checked to see whether it is feasible to produce it—and so on down the line. Different people may have to assume responsibility for each of these steps. Because there are so many steps and the responsibility for each step is taken by different people, some steps are often missed or else the relationship between steps is faulty. No one seems to assume an over-all responsibility for a major share of the work to make sure that the steps are coordinated. As a consequence, new products do not seem to meet deadlines. If they do, specifications are often incomplete or costly. At other times the specifications are complete, but the product turns out to be unsound customerwise. It may be advisable to organize by combining various steps by measurable results. If possible, try to assign over-all accountability for the total product development. If this can be done, the result is usually more efficiently accomplished.

We should point out that these problems are normal, even with sincere people trying to do a job, under these conditions. It is the basic setup on accountability that must be revised so that good people may work in a sound environment that more effectively encourages them to blend their work for best accomplishment.

In production, if a product is moved back and forth among quite a number of operators in the course of its manufacture, a good deal of time may be spent on handling, with little accountability for the over-all result of producing a finished product at a specified cost. In such a case it may be much sounder to combine operations and have one operator complete a number of them, including his own setup. If this cannot be done, it may at least be possible to have all related operations brought under one supervisor. In any event, it is usually wise to assign major measurable steps along the way to one individual or supervisor. You will ordinarily get much better control of the operation. The trend in many plants is counter to this—the attempt is made to break down all work by specialties. A constant series of arguments and extra movement between departments may result.

Accountability Need Not Be Unique

As we mentioned in Chapter 7, page 67, a result is rarely the consequence of only one man's action. If accountability is always considered to be unique—attributable to a single man—it tends to be inadequate. When a supervisor has just graduated from a group doing similar work to one where the work is dissimilar, his tendency to try to fix unique accountability for a result is apt to be strengthened. This approach is now even more inadequate because in the variable situation the work of one man is more likely to depend on another. There are many cases where two or more people must be held accountable for contributing part of the same result. In other words, there must be dual accountability. Since one man is contributing part of a result that is going to be incorporated in the result of another to arrive at the completed job, they must both be accountable in such a way that they will want to work together and will both be credited for getting the over-all result.

A supervisor will encounter resistance from his people when he sets up this type of accountability. A man may feel that it is unfair to hold him accountable when he does not have complete control of the total accomplishment. The supervisor must sell the necessity for this type of accountability even though full authority does not go with it. He must convince his men that such joint procedure must be the normal mode of operation. It is rare, anyway, that anyone has "complete" or "full" authority. Authority at best is authority within company policy. Particularly when the work is variable, authority is only partial. Even within company policy several people may have some responsibility for part of an over-all result. The basic question that should be asked is: "To what results does this man contribute?" Then *a man should be accountable in some way for the final results of all those items to which he is supposed to contribute in a major way.* The net effect of this rule is to make it advantageous for each individual to more thoroughly cooperate where it is necessary for the soundest over-all company operation. It tends to bring his personal objectives in line with those of the corporation.

Budgets Can Be Misleading

When a supervisor or manager has diversified positions under him and difficulty in measuring each part of the work, he very frequently turns to budget systems as a natural way to keep on top of diverse operations. Unfortunately, budgets are not always tied to sound company objectives and, in addition, do not always reflect the controllable areas that the man should be most accountable for. Therefore, budgets may not really be a control at all. For example, there may be heavy pressure to get more funds without specifying the expected consequence of the proposed increase in expenditures. Frequently people will demand a higher budget—all they can get—knowing that if they simply operate within the budget they are all right. Government operation is often understandably expensive for this reason. In diversified work it may be extremely difficult to pin down exactly how high a budget is justified. As a consequence, budgeting may become too loose.

Since in diversified work situations it often seems expensive to develop a budget that reflects the individual work of each person or supervisor, there is a tendency to combine operations recordwise in order to get a "workable" budget. Each individual may therefore lose some of the personal sense of accountability for taking constructive, positive action as soon as any deviation occurs. The budget plan itself may imply that he is not personally accountable since he does not control many of the items.

One of the major objections to budgets is that they only reflect cost. As we have pointed out earlier, the basic purpose of a record plan is to stimulate individuals to constructive action. We should never lose sight of the fact that the fundamental purpose of most jobs is to get creative results, not simply to control costs. Costs are always involved, but they are usually secondary and should be reviewed in the light of the results accomplished. It is highly important that this philosophy be sold to every individual. It tends to create a more farsighted and thinking individual in the job, one attuned to the corporate objectives.

13

Maintaining Individual Accomplishment from Variable Groups

WHAT ADDITIONAL DIFFICULTIES does a manager encounter when he is directing the work of several groups and the work of each group is different from that of the others? Is the application of management principles any different in this more complex setup?

To begin with, objectives are more difficult to set than when groups have similar work. In addition, more planning is required for coordinating these objectives and holding people to account in a harmonious way. Delegation is more complex, because more attention must be given to logical combinations of activities and to the development of sound relationships between dissimilar operations. Larger staff services frequently spring up without making a commensurate contribution to the firm's objectives.

There is a natural tendency for managers to assume that procedures that were successful previously will apply to this more complex setup in the same way.

SPECIFY RESULTS FOR THE GROUP

As far as possible, the principle of specialization referred to in Chapter 11, page 122, should be applied. *Require only one specialized skill of each group if the group can be made accountable for a complete result.* It is difficult to train men to do several different kinds of work well. Mistakes often repeat themselves if the original delegation of results did not recognize the principle of specialization as fully as it might have. The problem is accentuated when a company has many new employees. The supervisors have difficulty teaching the whole job because there is too much for the new employee to learn within a given time. Training cannot be completed on time, so a variety of methods (many of them poor) spring into use and sloppy habits develop.

Problems of relationship are also intensified with a number of variable groups. One person, or group, tends to be dependent on another and may be held up because of the poor work or poor timing of the other. Individuals are often unaware of all the ramifications of their work and seem to give little attention to their effect on others. A manager may feel that his people lack a cooperative spirit. One solution is to *keep operations that are in sequence within one group.* In this way the manager can hold one supervisor accountable for the total result. The supervisor cannot "pass the buck" by saying that he had to wait for someone else to get something ready for him. In addition, you will minimize the number of cross relationships between supervisors. The communication requirements are reduced, with all the possibilities of misunderstanding inherent in the written or spoken word. The number of coordinating meetings will also be reduced, along with the extra bickering that might occur between supervisors.

Related to this principle of keeping sequential items together is the problem of dependent functions. When one person depends on another for a service, or skill, in order to get a job done, it is only natural that he tends to blame the other if anything goes wrong. If a foreman does not supervise material handling, he is inclined to blame the material-handling group for problems in meeting schedules. In a supermarket chain all specialists may report directly to the home office. The district manager is then inclined to be critical and blame the home office specialists for poorly run departments in the stores. If all the various sections of a government office that combine to give a particular service are placed under a regional manager, he can be made more solidly accountable for net results from that region. *When one function depends on another in order to complete its result, both of them should be under the same supervisor* if at all possible.

This principle may suggest a partial breakup of a service function, however. It may be highly advantageous to take that part of the service function that works entirely for one department and attach it to the supervisor of that department. In this way he has complete control of both servicing and operations. Phases of the work in material handling, machine scheduling, and maintenance departments may lend themselves to this approach. In a large plant, this breakup of service functions and allocation to the departments serviced may be feasible for many services, but the assignment of the function may have to be made at the second or third management echelon in the line.

Let the Supervisor Do It

At the stage of management where several groups report to a manager on a variety of work, the manager himself must exercise greater personal discipline than in simpler setups. He should determine the delegation of results to his supervisors. However, *supervisors should organize their own groups;* the manager should refrain from doing this for them. Ordinarily the supervisors are closer to the problems. This approach tends to sharpen up the accountability of each supervisor. He will develop better if he is required to think through his own delegation in the light of the results expected of him. In addition it lays the groundwork for the application of the exception principle and relieves the manager of knowing the details of every little operation under him.

Managers frequently err in this regard. It is natural for them to want to determine the specific organization for each supervisor because they feel they are more experienced. If they do this, however, supervisors will not feel fully accountable for the accomplishment of their men. When a general manager or a president attempts too actively to organize the divisions below him for his key executives, he may wind up with a group of "yes men" and find himself continually solving their problems.

In order to maintain an over-all control, it may be helpful if the manager requires a supervisor to clear an organization plan with him before its installation. This review must be tactfully done, however, because the accountability even of an experienced supervisor can be weakened in the process. The supervisor may feel that he is really not defining his own organization, since he must clear with someone above. He may be very hesitant about making any changes required to meet the situations that face him. The "approved" organization plan tends to become rigid, leading to an excessive rigidity in the outlook of the supervisor himself.

BLEND THE DIFFERENT TYPES OF WORK

Accountability is more difficult to establish for several groups doing a variety of work than when their work is similar. There are more interrelationships between people and it is harder to get accurate measurements of results. Authority may then be set up unrealistically. Over-all, the requirements for coordination of the groups are more demanding. Timing now becomes critical, especially in one of the faster, more mechanized industries. (Timing problems have been aggravated, in any case, because of the great improvements in communications and transportation that have occurred throughout the world, making service and supplier problems more critical.) The specification of *timing required should be part of the delegation of results from every manager to his supervisors.* You can readily see the advisability of tying a function to those that serve it or to those in the same result sequence. Tie-in timing becomes easier since it is then the direct responsibility of one supervisor. The problem is pushed to a primary level, usually a more efficient setup.

How should a manager approach effective delegation of results to several groups when the work is variable? As pointed up in Chapter 11, page 131, one practical way is for the manager to *build* his *delegation around the critical requirements of his operation.* He should carefully analyze his total operation in order to pin down the make-or-break items, the important or critical points around which other operations tend to flow. (There may be two or three or more such critical requirements.) He should then delegate to his supervisors in the light of these critical requirements. Key jobs will then tend to get done, necessary details are not missed as often, and unnecessary details are not given excessive attention.

For example, some plants give most of their attention to assembly operations, because the bulk of the work is done there. However, foundry and certain machining processes may precede the assembly and critically affect the whole operation. In that case the organization definition must place important weight on getting the most effective timing and dependable quality from these departments.

A printing firm may have developed excellent relations with a limited number of large accounts. There is a tendency to concentrate attention on keeping these customers. (And of course this concern is logical; the firm should certainly want to hold on to them.) However, comparatively little effort is put into the development of new accounts, another critical area. As a consequence, the firm may hold relatively steady over a period of years even though it is in an accelerated-growth industry. In a period of slump this weakness will show up with a vengeance, particularly should one of these old-time accounts fold up or be inclined to do a closer buying job.

We should emphasize one point in regard to delegating by critical requirements. The manager should ordinarily delegate the responsibility for only one critical requirement to each supervisor. A common error is to delegate the responsibility for all critical requirements, or most of them, to one supervisor. A weakened operation, long-run, usually results. Should any problem occur in this supervisor's area, he may not be able to carry through on all the critical areas. In effect, the manager is not depending as fully as he should on each of his key supervisors.

Do Not Build around One Supervisor

When a manager is attempting to blend different kinds of work, he may naturally gravitate toward dependence on his best supervisor. The same weaknesses in delegation then develop that were pointed up in the simpler supervisory setup discussed on page 130. The implications for the organization are greater, however, because you are dealing with results of more far-reaching consequence to the firm. Building your organization structure around an individual at this level can leave large gaps in accountability. Since delegations have not been made logically by results, it is easy for activities that are absolutely necessary to remain undelegated. Major imbalances can develop. The weakness may be particularly evident when a key man around whom the organization has been designed is replaced. The new man may be unable to handle the full responsibility of his predecessor. In this kind of organization setup a job change is a major problem.

The situation usually develops because the manager feels that he cannot trust his supervisors to delegate properly. He may not fully recognize that the Rule of Errors applies to supervisory positions just as well as to lower-level jobs—that you have to expect a certain number of errors as part of normal operation, even as part of outstanding performance. One reason why the manager may not be placing reliance on some of his supervisors is that he just will not accept deviations as part of normal operation. The error at this level looms too large to him. (The problem is aggravated as you go farther up the line.) Once the manager fully recognizes the necessity of a tolerance for error for each of his operations, it is surprising how rarely he has to build organization structure around individuals. Men come through.

Develop Harmony between Groups

If the manager has delegated soundly, *results defined for one group should be harmonious with those defined for another.* (This principle is similar, of course, to that of the importance of having harmonious objectives between people within the group, discussed earlier.) If they are not harmonious, he will be constantly engaged in arbitrating or in ferreting out obstacles to the smooth blending of different parts of his operation. He may have a constant flow of "rush" items. These may occur because his original delegation was not thought through to provide harmonious timing between groups. In some cases the results expected of one group may be completely interwoven with those of another. It is natural for the manager to try to set up one group independently of another, but the accomplishment required of the various groups may make this impossible if they are to be harmonious with each other.

In an architectural firm the engineering layouts for a certain project may not blend with the basic architectural design either functionally or aesthetically. The net results expected from each group must be set up so that the engineering and the architectural groups work together toward the best building for the client, blending the functional, cost, and aesthetic points of view.

Some plants are not made accountable for meeting schedules that the customers require. Only costs are emphasized. As a consequence the sales department may be severely handicapped in making delivery commitments in a particularly competitive market. Since the prime emphasis in the plant has been on cost, perhaps through a tight budget system, it is only natural that the supervisors give less attention to the more remote question of delivery, particularly when special employee, material, or equipment problems give them good excuses for not meeting schedules.

How would a manager know whether the results expected of one department are harmonious with those of another? It should be advantageous to both groups to work toward company results. In other words, people will cooperate much better when each one gets credit for the accomplishment through sound accountability. The manager must trace through the relationship until he is satisfied that this is true. To the extent that men or groups are in effect working against each other, you tend to get disharmony between them. It is then easy to conclude that the people concerned are just naturally not cooperative or loyal, which probably is not true. A strong department may get the ascendancy and reach out beyond its area of responsibility—a perfectly natural thing for a strong supervisor to do. Additional imbalance develops, requiring more and more attention from the manager.

Be Watchful of Committees

Because of the complex and interwoven nature of the problems involved in getting a blending of different kinds of work, a manager may quite naturally go overboard on committee operation. Since coordination seems to be of major importance, all attention is focused on getting cooperation and better communication. It is easy, however, for the committee operation to encourage a relaxation of accountability. There is a natural tendency for an employee to bring his problems to the group and to feel less accountable for the result when the group agrees on a solution.

Committees also tend to encourage a flourishing "paper mill." All kinds of reports seem necessary (with many copies) in order to "inform" all the interested parties. In many cases, if a supervisor read all the reports he received he would have no time to do anything else. The excessive development of reports resulting from committee meetings should be a red flag to any manager that the committees may be replacing personal accountability. After all, if everyone is informed, can anyone be very critical of the result?

In addition, "coordinating" meetings often tend to be post-mortems. Committees leave much to be desired as a means of effectively blending different kinds of work. If a series of committees are constantly necessary, it could be an indication to the manager that his delegation of results to each of his supervisors has not been carefully thought out so that the results expected are harmonious with each other. Or it might suggest that the individual supervisors do not feel a personal sense of accountability. If delegations are sound, far fewer meetings are necessary, and when such meetings do occur, they usually involve fewer people.

Set Specific Growth Objectives

When a firm engages in many different kinds of work, the problem of obtaining the balanced growth of the company becomes more complicated. There is a tendency for certain parts to grow irrespective of other parts. Growth in one area of a company may in some instances occur in a direction entirely antagonistic to that of another area. *If growth is an objective of the company, planning for growth should also be part of the delegation to each supervisor.* You may ask, "How do you include this planning for growth?" In defining the results for the supervisor, include objectives for those things that will build the operation for the future. In sales this may mean new accounts, new product volume, balanced coverage, or new territories. In a construction firm special emphasis may be required on type and volume of estimating and on cost build-ups to enable the firm to be more competitive in a variety of construction jobs.

Whenever a manager finds that unanticipated problems are constantly occurring as the firm grows, that men do not seem capable of meeting new challenges, and that parts of the business are too inflexible to meet new conditions brought on by growth, the chances are that he has not delegated results that forced planning for company growth.

COORDINATE WORK OF SUPERVISORS

When there is great variation in the types of activities being performed, it is difficult for each supervisor to maintain an effective tie-in with the work of other supervisors. Little kingdoms start to develop—isolated groups more concerned with their own activity than with the success of the enterprise. Ambitious empire builders spring up; individual groups do not carry through completely on their basic responsibilities. The manager's action may be partly at fault. In delegating, he may not have fully appreciated the importance of good supervision, its impact on accomplishment, and the setup required to make it work.

Span of Control—All Clear-cut Responsibilities

It is extremely difficult for supervisors to coordinate with each other if their personal responsibilities are not clear. To the extent that the manager spells out a clear-cut responsibility for all the work he delegates he expands his own span of control. It is easier for him to effectively supervise his supervisors. The more the "gray" areas of delegation, the fewer men a man can supervise. He will have to be in on more problems and have more meetings in order to "coordinate." While this problem is similar to that of defining results for individuals when work becomes complex and develops more echelons, the manager will find this more elaborate delegation quite difficult and be inclined to spend less time than he should to define clear-cut responsibilities for his supervisors. If delegation to supervisors is fuzzy, it militates against clear-cut delegation of responsibilities by the supervisors to their people, leading to an even greater supervisory requirement on the part of the manager.

Span of Control—Complexity of Operation

But there are other factors to be considered in determining the span of control for individual supervisors. The work may be of greater complexity than formerly. More training is then required for each person, and it is more difficult to set objectives and hold people accountable. Gaps in training are more likely to occur and unexpected errors to pop up. *A supervisor supervising complex work cannot handle as many people as on simple work.* The manager must consider this when he delegates responsibility to his supervisors—fewer people must be assigned to the individual supervisor.

Span of Control—Variability of Operation

When all the work is similar, it is easier to supervise. Objectives are easier to set; training is simplified; accountability is less of a problem. *If the work being supervised is variable, the supervisor or manager cannot supervise as many people.* It is more difficult to be close to all the work and to understand all the requirements. Frequently there is less back-up for a job.

If the work under his supervisors is variable, the manager cannot delegate as much responsibility to each supervisor and expect it to be fully carried out. At the same time, however, because of this variability, he must delegate more authority to his supervisors and spend more of his own time on over-all coordination (his own span of control is more limited). Variability is often the reason why chief executives have a very limited span of effective control. Each of the functions under them is completely different from the other functions. A plant division may be affected if each department within the division is essentially different from every other one, particularly if there is a great deal of job shop work. The span of control of a manager of a department store may be affected if the store sells many types of products, caters to different types of customers, and also operates by mail order. The variability usually means that he cannot effectively supervise more than a limited number of employees.

Span of Control—Critical Function

A related factor for the manager to consider is the degree to which the functions he is supervising are of a critical nature (those in which one error might result in a great deal of loss). *Having many critical areas under his direction limits his span of control.* Conversely, however, it usually means that he must delegate more to an individual supervisor because spot decisions of some consequence must be made during the day-to-day operation. This is a common occurrence in a critical function.

When functions are critical, the manager's supervisors, in turn, must also have fewer people reporting to them. Otherwise they may be too busy with unimportant items to cover the timing requirements of the critical functions and meet emergency situations as they arise. Considering the amount at stake, this could be disastrous.

Examples might be the operation of an explosive plant or of any manufacturing process where a short period of inattention might have serious consequences. When a plant changes to automation, the effect of any one error can be greatly increased. Extreme care must be exercised to be sure that the supervisor does not exceed his span of control, so that he can quickly handle the difficult problems at the time they occur.

In a new operation critical functions are difficult to determine until after the shakedown period. More supervision than usual must be provided, because for a period of time a number of functions may be critical. Breaking into a new territory or a new area like a foreign country may have similar implications. It is difficult to foresee the critical problems, so supervisors must not be overloaded. They must have the flexibility to be able to meet these problems when they occur.

Span of Control—New vs. *Experienced Management Employees*

We pointed out in Chapter 9, page 102, that a supervisor's span of control is limited if he has many new or inexperienced people. As you go up the line the effect is greater. New or inexperienced management employees usually have little loyalty to the operation and a limited understanding of its basic mode of operation or of its objectives. Since the manager must depend on these supervisors to lead their men, he must spend considerable time training them and handling what would be difficult problems for them. *With new management people, a manager cannot supervise as many supervisors.* Both the manager and each of his supervisors may have to shorten their span of control so that better attention can be given to training each supervisor in management philosophy and practice. In the long run, the total time required to bring the whole operation to a reasonable level of operation and to a reasonable cost is usually reduced by this limitation. If both the supervisor and his men are new, the problem increases.

The manager must recognize that in most cases the immediate supervisor, whether new or not, is still the primary trainer of his people. The supervisor can usually train more effectively if he is able to do the subordinate jobs himself. If he has never done them, adequate time and attention must be given to training him first. If a new supervisor has so many people reporting to him that he is unable to train in new people, train older people in new methods, and learn all jobs himself, poor operation will probably result, together with a great many employee problems. New methods and new installations will not move and individual people will appear unwilling to cooperate fully. The basic problem may be inadequately applied first-line supervision.

Some executives say the primary ability a supervisor needs is skill in handling people. They therefore make the mistake, when they select supervisors, of assuming that this is the only requirement. However, first-line supervisors must be equipped to train in their people and point the way to sound methods. Employees respect their supervisors much more when they feel that they are technically competent. For that matter, how can a first-line supervisor follow up and hold his men accountable if he himself is not completely familiar with the requirements of the operation? He does not have to be perfect at the work, but he should usually be able to do a reasonable job. This requirement holds just as true for the district sales manager as it does for the foreman or the project supervisor in a laboratory. Companies often lag when they are trying to expand rapidly with new people because they fail to recognize this. They have not understood the training requirement in supervision.

ENCOURAGE THE TOTAL RESULT

When the number of different jobs under his supervision increases, the manager has increasing difficulty in maintaining his perspective. It is comparatively easy to focus on all the minor errors and problems that occur and lose sight of the over-all results that should be obtained. Each of these little problems can be seen all by itself. Each seems to be something which can be corrected and which would merit some attention. As a consequence, a manager may tend to put more and more strings on his supervisors in an attempt to correct each minor problem. He may become more aware of the individual cost of each error than he is of the total accumulation of errors as weighed against results. At times the total of these errors may seem so overwhelming that he tightens up on authority, stifling the initiative of the supervisors. As a consequence he restricts accomplishment. The lack of accomplishment, in turn, seems justification for tightening authority even more—the manager has just proved that his tightening of authority was justified. The whole process encourages poor operation.

A manager must *broaden authority for supervisors when operations are variable.* There is a contrary tendency to be more careful about giving authority in order to be on top of all the different areas. Because of the variability, however, the manager finds this more difficult than it was when all the work was similar. In practice the manager must rely more heavily on the individual initiative of his supervisors. More authority to decide procedure should be delegated to them. When this is done, supervisors usually demonstrate a considerable degree of ingenuity in solving their own problems, and fewer questions have to come up the line.

Good Records Are Necessary

When the work is variable, the problem of developing records on accomplishment in each area often appears to be insurmountable. It just does not seem as if a record system that gets down to each small area could possibly pay for itself. However, if it does not get down to each area, accountability for each small area will not be pinned down to an individual. Frequently records will only show an over-all result of several supervisors or management men. Their primary utility seems to be the presenting of negative reports up the line on some over-all deviation. The individual supervisors then become somewhat lukewarm toward any kind of record.

If the records do not adequately point up the responsibility of each supervisor, each may tend to blame another for lack of accomplishment instead of focusing on ways of preventing the problem in the future. In many cases it is better to have the controller *help the man or the supervisor develop his own records.* A supervisor is more likely to use records that he keeps himself. When the work is quite variable, it is also more difficult for the controller to understand all the parts of the operation sufficiently to adequately interpret records. In addition, records kept by the supervisor are almost always current, and he is usually much more willing to accept their accuracy. A word of caution, however: The controller must develop some method of recording deviations when they are beyond the authority of the supervisor. Otherwise the manager may not have adequate control of the operation.

There are always some parts of variable work on which it is extremely hard to keep records. A start can be made in developing a sense of accountability in supervision if you *keep records on certain portions of a job even though records are not temporarily available on other portions.* Many people feel that when only part of a job can be measured at any one time (a common problem when there is a great variability in the work), no measurement at all should be attempted. This is a fallacy. It is usually worthwhile keeping records on those parts that can be measured so that supervisors become accustomed to this mode of operation. It builds greater insight and a better sense of accountability. During the period of partial recording it becomes easier to develop other records to cover the other results expected of the supervisor.

As we have stated earlier, no man should have authority or be allowed to exercise influence unless he is accountable for the effect of that authority or influence. When the work is variable, this effect is sometimes quite difficult to trace. A record should be devised, however, that reflects the positive or negative effect of this influence, even though it does it crudely.

A typical example may occur in an appliance store. The salesman has the primary influence on the customer. It may be advisable to make him accountable for profit on his sales, and records should be kept accordingly. He can then be charged with the losses on trade-ins. But note this: He should have the right to decide whether or not he should take the trade-in and to determine its value (at least within limits). Under these circumstances he is likely to be judicious in the exercise of this authority.

14

True Management Control Bypasses the Executive

In the previous chapters we have periodically touched on the part that the record system can play in creating an invigorating management climate. This part is so great that it is advantageous to explore the various ramifications of records systems, or control, more fully as they affect the management process. Accounting reports and records are usually set up to provide financial information on the operation of a business. This has always been an essential for the owners or managers of any business to help them in their over-all planning. A chief executive feels he has to know whether all the straggling tentacles of his operation finally blend into an over-all result that is satisfactory. Accounting reports and records contribute substantially to the knowledge of the executive who would otherwise be removed from the actual operation of the business. It is perfectly natural for these reports to be designed to inform the top executives. Unfortunately, this design tends to force a greater and greater centralization of authority. The inevitable consequence is to discourage enterprising decision making at subordinate management levels.

Let us assume that the objective of management control is to stimulate corrective action promptly on any deviation adverse to the objectives of the enterprise. Accounting philosophy is often inadequate in that it is not based on sound management insight as to what makes men work or create. There is a real danger that it may not view an operation as a dynamic, ever-changing, striving enterprise of thinking men. As a consequence, records may not be viewed as management tools that should be utilized throughout the operation to aid and abet the creative initiative of the whole management team at every level of the enterprise, including every management position (vice-presidents, foremen, salesmen, engineers, personnel directors, sales managers, office supervisors, etc.).

How can records be utilized to provide a sound management tool for stimulating accomplishment throughout the enterprise?

FUNDAMENTALS OF CONTROL

To start off, a supervisor or manager should determine objectives for a period for his man [(1), Figure 9]. In addition, as we discussed earlier, he should ask himself the questions leading to the definition of the authority limits for the man [(2), Figure 9]. At the same time, the supervisor should set up a basis for holding the man accountable at the end of the period for the accomplishment of these objectives [(3), Figure 9]. (The Time Period on Figure 9 indicates the period for which the objectives have been set—six months, one year, etc.) It is only then that management control comes into prominence. It should be the function of whoever keeps the records to record any deviations (indicated by the dots in Figure 9) from a trend in the

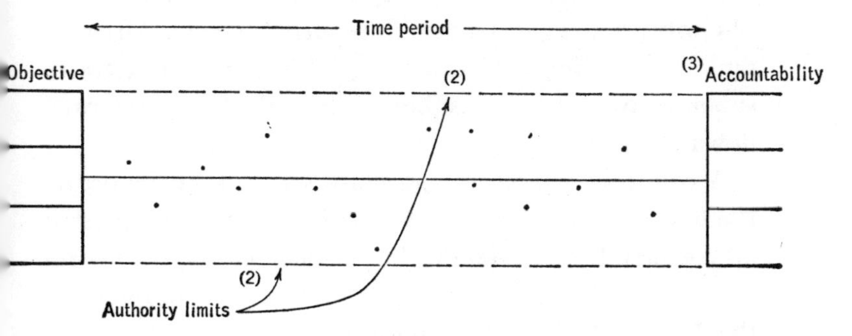

FIG. 9 Action control.

direction of accomplishment of these objectives, with the idea of stimulating corrective action on the part of the man under control, so that he can arrive at the final over-all accomplishment of his objectives. First off, then, a *sound management control system is aimed at stimulating action.* The very purpose is different from that of typical accounting reports. As a consequence, the format of the reports, the way they are amassed and presented, is often different. This fundamental difference in philosophy is important for a manager to recognize in setting up a sound management control system.

It is important to go further, however. Accounting normally gives a "general" report on conditions. It is aimed at giving an over-all picture, notwithstanding the detailed information often used to do this. A management control system, on the other hand, should *focus on deviations from objectives*—objectives that have been set for each management man for a particular period. It should point up deviations that require some attention. It should not be greatly concerned with presenting voluminous statistical data. It could very well be, for example, that an executive has only a few figures a month reported to him. All other figures, outlining deviations or problems which relate to subobjectives of other subordinates, would be reported down the line.

Accounting needs are normally satisfied by reporting the figures. The primary purpose is to accurately present all the data. It is natural for the person amassing the figures to take an attitude that it is up to someone else to interpret the figures. "The information is all there." Executives should bear in mind, however, that this approach imposes a heavy burden upon other members of the operation, particularly non-figure-minded people such as sales managers or first-line supervisors. In addition, the reports are frequently so long that the hard-working line executive just does not have the time to ferret out the significant figures in the mass of detail presented. This could occur at almost any level. A typical example was a budget report that was issued for one division of a company. This one budget alone included 65 solid pages of figures.

Since the primary objective of a management control system is that of stimulating action, it is basic that the *controller creatively interpret the figures.* Who should know better the meaning of the figures than the man who amassed them? Very often a significant item strikes him immediately because of his familiarity with the figures. Instead of merely presenting the over-all reports, he should give interpretations of these significant implications so that action may be taken by the man under control. The whole approach will often lead to a significant change in the manner of reporting. Sometimes a one-sentence statement describing the implications of a figure is more effective than a ten-page report.

It is fairly apparent that the controller or figure man must be reasonably conversant with the work of the line. Usually he must be near them physically in order to understand their problems so that he can adequately interpret the figures. Physical remoteness is one of the inherent weaknesses of going too far on centralized accounting, efficient though it may seem in the utilization of equipment.

One of the dangers of most record systems is that they quite naturally tend to focus on costs. The record system itself very frequently results from top management's interest in controlling runaway costs. As we pointed out earlier, this cost focus may easily occur, for example, in a budget program. A typical line supervisor or manager often gets the feeling that if he fights for a higher budget and merely keeps within the budget he has done the job. Note the implications. This does not push creative work, new developments, new methods, or improvements in operations. As a matter of fact, it tends to militate against them. Creative work usually requires gambles, gambles which may show up negatively in the cost figures presented in the budgets or other accounting reports. Even a so-called flexible budget system frequently misses this point. In the eyes of the supervisor it takes so much explanation to get an OK of a change that he gives up. Frequently he wishes to experiment. Any explanation he makes before he has tried something may sound weak. An executive must give this human factor careful consideration if he wishes to keep the record system from drying up the innate initiative of his management team all the way down the line.

A management control system develops records on all objectives. And this is the key! Creative management objectives may often be more important than cost objectives. After all, is not the fundamental purpose of most positions to create something rather than to simply control costs? Every manager must keep this in mind. In addition, a true management control plan should focus on improvement. It should encourage records that report improvement in operation which may or may not show up immediately in cost reduction. This focus may require an entirely different approach in the ways records are developed. It has pointed implications, for example, in sales and product development departments. In sales, emphasis may be needed on new accounts, on new product volume, or on partial territorial results. Product development, in turn, may need a long-term new-product-return approach to be significant.

Because of the history of accounting reports (and perhaps the natural inclination of the staff man to report up the line) accounting reports tend to go to the higher executives. Frequently little at all is reported to the first-line management. There is a tacit assumption that first-line supervisors are really not part of management. The comment is also made that "it's too expensive to develop records on every small breakdown." The accounting department then becomes a kind of supersleuth ferreting out errors and pointing them up to higher executives. It may do little creatively to help the man down the line to appreciate his own operation; traditionally this has not been its function. Quite the reverse should be true, however, if you want a management control plan to act as a stimulating tool throughout the operation. *The control plan should report deviations to the management man himself, **not** to his superior.* As long as the deviation is within the man's authority, he should first have a chance to correct the problem. Frequently this is the point where action should be taken. You can readily see the importance of being realistic about setting broad authority limits. In addition, the record system must be devised so that it reports the deviation before it goes beyond the man's authority (a condition not usually characteristic of accounting reports). However, the executive or manager must require some over-all control. When the deviation is beyond the authority of the man, it should be reported to his superior.

There is a natural reluctance on the part of an executive to have "outside" record people go directly to his subordinates and not to him. He must adjust to a different mode of operation. Under normal conditions little would now be reported to the manager or executive above. He would, therefore, be freer to work on broader problems. At the same time he would be assured (more so than had formerly been the case) that a significant deviation would come to his attention, so that he would in effect retain adequate control of his operation. This approach forces a decentralization of authority and generally creates a much more satisfactory relationship between the control man and the line man. The control man is now a helper rather than a finger pointer. It is his job to apprise the man under control of a deviation so that he himself can correct it, and be finally recognized for sound achievement by his superior at the end of the period. In this way a management control system provides one of the strongest factors available for building a strong over-all management sense in people all the way down the line. It develops stronger responsible people at all levels.

Another obstacle to sound management control is the fact that accounting reports tend to be standard year after year, in line with the careful, methodical thinking required in most accounting systems. It tends to give order to the system and does, of course, have the decided advantage of facilitating a comparison from one period to another, an important function of many reports. From a management control point of view, however, considerable added value may be obtained by making reports more flexible. In a dynamic economy such as ours, the objectives that should be set for management men up and down the line should probably change every year, as needs change, organizations change, conditions change, emphasis changes. *Reporting systems for management control should change automatically with changes in objectives.* In other words, for the greatest stimulation a management control system must be flexible. Reports for one period may vary substantially from the reports that were issued the year before. This flexibility is fundamental when you look at the overall objective of management control—that of stimulating men to the action, constructive action, required in a particular period.

According to sound accounting principles any expense is usually charged to only one department; it is thought inappropriate to even consider charging a cost item in total to more than one department. How, say the accountants, could you have a balanced accounting system if you did this? From the standpoint of management control, however, this traditional accounting thinking has grave weaknesses. It presupposes that every responsibility is completely independent of every other one. In most cases this is not true in any normal operation. As we pointed out earlier, the theory of unique accountability just does not hold.

For example, there are almost always overlaps between a typical staff function and a line function that it serves, in terms of the results they are intended to effect. (The staff man is usually set up to help the line man do some portion of his work better.) Timing decisions made by a sales department may greatly increase the cost of production. Unless the result of these decisions is charged against sales as well as production they are exercising authority without being held accountable—usually not sound management. In pointing up deviations from objectives, therefore, *a management control system may charge the same item to two or more people.* Several people may be given full credit or full discredit for the same result. This double charging is necessary to pound home a full sense of accountability for the total result. In addition you have devised a setup that makes it advantageous for men to cooperate with each other, generally a more effective incentive, as has been pointed out, than frequent exhortations to "cooperate" and be good company men.

One limitation to this rule is that you should not charge a man with items that have no relationship to his work. Such accounting will appear unfair to him and usually reduces the stimulus. Budgets often suffer in this way—a man is charged with items over which he has practically no control. He loses confidence in the whole budget system and its incentive value is considerably reduced.

You may ask, "How can you ever get the duplication involved out of your accounting system?" In general, it can be done rather simply with washout accounts which can be set up to balance out for final statement purposes. From a sound control point of view it is important that this double (or triple) charging be done so that you can maintain the stimulating effect of reporting deviations from objectives to the man concerned.

PRINCIPLES TO MAKE MANAGEMENT CONTROLS WORK

One of the difficulties encountered in using normal accounting reports to stimulate management is that they tend to report all deviations indiscriminately. They frequently make no differentiation between statistically random deviations and significant deviations (those with an underlying cause). From the point of view of accounting theory the difference may not be important. However, look at this from an action point of view. There is no purpose at all in disturbing management people about random deviations. You can't cry "Wolf" all of the time. There are normal fluctuations in any operation that tend to balance out over a period of time. Focusing attention on them tends to restrict authority limits in that the man becomes worried about every small deviation. A management control system that acts as a stimulus to constructive action should *focus only on significant deviations.* The focus on significant deviations will strengthen management-by-exception and will allow the management control system to contribute significantly to the broader development of the management people under control.

From the point of view of action the most common weakness of accounting reports is that they are usually summaries after the fact. They are primarily static in nature. They may be anywhere from two to eight weeks late —frequently far too late to take any constructive action. *Above all, a management control system must be current!* This currency is critical if your aim is to stimulate action in time. But how current must they be? The reports should indicate a deviation at the first instance of significant deviation and (this is important) while the deviation is still within the man's authority. Reporting may be required for periods of two weeks, one week, or even daily. The determining factor is that information should be issued before the deviation is beyond the man's authority. Because of the timing required, a major change may be needed to broaden accounting reports, as typically developed, so that they become effective management controls.

The difficulty is that the currency required may appear almost impossible to develop without an inordinate amount of work. One of the major reasons for this is that the accuracy needed for financial reports develops the natural tendency to carry all reports out to two decimal places. This emphasis on accuracy is a major stumbling block in carrying over to a true management control approach. Let us go back to our fundamental objective—that of stimulating constructive management action. Most management decisions are not based on data of extreme accuracy. All that a manager wants to know is that there is a significant deviation. *Frequently crude estimates will be adequate* for this purpose (perhaps even 10 or 20 per cent in error). This philosophy changes the whole approach to record systems when they are adapted to control purposes. It permits a much easier amassing of figures. "Guesstimates" are often satisfactory. A management control system becomes possible where at first it would appear to be impossible because of the extreme accuracy normally required by accounting systems.

Because of this supposed accuracy requirement, many controllers have felt that they could not have a control system such as we have described unless they have highly developed, mechanized record systems. Considering the crude estimates that may be permitted, there are many firms that would not need refined mechanization in order to maintain a sound management control system. In actual practice this "accuracy" is more or less illusory anyway. You often find that the 10-digit figures commonly reported were the result of an overhead allocation multiple estimated only to the second digit. It is difficult to understand how accuracy to 10 digits could be expected from multiplying a figure with only 1-digit accuracy.

Because of their familiarity with figures, accountants and controllers develop a superficial insight into every facet of the business. It is easy for them to succumb to the illusion that they alone understand the intricate workings of every part of the company. They therefore frequently try to point out the specific course of action that the line man should take, failing to realize that almost invariably they are not qualified to do this. They often have the ear of higher management, however, and thus may inject a serious organization weakness into the setup in that they are assuming authority by pointed suggestions which are given considerable weight but are not accountable for the consequences. A controller's management recommendation has frequently proved a hindrance rather than a help to sound management action. In many cases a militant controller, sincere though he may have been, has done more basic harm than any other executive in the firm. On the other hand, *true management control should interpret the figures and point out the area where action is needed. The action itself is determined by the line man.* In other words, the control plan should simply point out the problem area and interpret the meaning of the figures. The decision as to what kind of action should be taken, if any, should always be up to the line man. As soon as the man keeping the records starts pointing out what should be done, he usurps supervision and may easily lead the line people astray. Since he has the figures, it is often difficult for the line man to argue with him. A supervisor may be encouraged to be a nonaggressive man whose prime purpose is "to keep his nose clean."

Another difficulty with making typical accounting plans work as controls is that they frequently use averages of many items as the most practical way to allocate costs—an easier method for arriving at over-all figures (completely distributed). In a management control system, however, these allocations should be broken down realistically wherever possible, by estimates if necessary—*records must reflect individual responsibilities.* It is important that the man under control have a major influence on the result that is reported to him. If much of the figure has been developed by general allocation, he does not feel that he personally can control the result. An example might be a plant-overhead allocation including substantial depreciation, maintenance, and engineering costs applied in the same way to a machining department as to an assembly department. Another example is the use of dollar volume as a basis for distributing order-handling, administrative, selling, or advertising expenses for two product lines that are radically different in size of order, number of items per order, type of customer, and geographical distribution of customers. From a control point of view the figures or interpretations may have little value. You tend to get alibis and the shrugging off of responsibility instead of responsible action.

MANAGEMENT SETUP REQUIRED FOR GOOD MANAGEMENT CONTROL

We should review some basic management approaches that are needed in order to get maximum value from a management control system. The first and fundamental point is that *management should be operating by objectives* (even though they are crude) *all the way down the line.* You can readily see the need for objectives that are specific, measurable results, not areas of action or activities. It is very difficult to develop a good control system that reports deviations back to the man when no standard or objective has been set for him in the first place. Authority limits become elastic. We believe that this is one reason why accounting has often failed to advance to sound management control. The very management setups in the companies have made good control difficult.

In addition, *objectives should be current.* Unless management changes its objectives every year with changes in conditions, significant deviations will not be meaningful to the man operating on the job. The reporting becomes out of date.

We should point out that accountants or controllers should not set objectives, as in effect they frequently do in budget setting by the very way they present data and top management thinking to other management people. *It is the job of the superior to set objectives* and, in addition, the limits of authority within which the man makes decisions. It is fairly obvious, of course, that this will be done better if it starts at the top. At the end of the period the man's superior—**not** the controller—should hold him accountable for total accomplishment (see (3), Figure 9).

In order to get men to take action *there must be a realistic decentralization of authority.* In other words, people down the line must be allowed to make the normal decisions, including normal errors, that would be required to accomplish the objectives set for them. If this is not the case, there is little point in reporting deviations to them. They are not in a position to step out and take action anyway. Permitting tolerance for the errors involved requires discipline on the part of other executives above. They must allow people down the line to take the action needed to correct the deviation reported by the control system. We are saying, in effect, that there must be a realistic recognition by top management of the management-by-exception principle **in application.**

Fundamentally, however, controllers and accountants must be accountable by the action principle. *A record man should be accountable for corrective action resulting from his records, not for the accumulation of records or for the presentation of reports as such.* He would not, in this case, be given any credit for the number, size, or completeness of reports, as is typically the case. In fact these would be looked at as charges against him, expense items. The only way in which he would get any credit at all would be by the action resulting from his reports. In other words, he should be tied very closely to the corrective action taken by the line people on whom he is keeping controls—corrective action toward all objectives, not just toward cost objectives. This is an entirely new approach to the responsibility of accounting people. At first they might be inclined to shrug off any such suggestion ("Action is the responsibility of the line"), but they would be shrugging off one of the greatest opportunities for contribution to company welfare that can be obtained from a record system. This approach merely recognizes a basic reason for the record function—to stimulate sound management action. Check the action resulting!

15

When Is Staff Profitable?

FAIRLY EARLY in the growth of any operation, the need arises for giving line people special service in certain areas. Let us define a staff man as "any man who must make his contribution to the flow of work of the enterprise through someone else who does not report to him or to one of his subordinates." Line men, on the other hand, are those who work directly in providing the result for which the enterprise is set up. In general, a line man is engaged in the circle of work that is absolutely necessary to provide the service or product of a firm, while a staff man assists in some way to provide this service or product in a better or cheaper way. In most firms typical line jobs are those of salesmen, sales managers, plant machine operators, foremen, and plant managers. Typical staff jobs might be those of cost analysts, personnel men, methods engineers, and advertising men. The latter rely on others to make their contribution to the objectives of the firm. What is a staff job in one institution, however, may be a line job in another, depending upon the basic service provided by the institution.

Watch the Growth of Staff

Staff usually grows more, proportionately, than the firm does. Staff often grows geometrically as against an arithmetical expansion of the line. The expedited growth of knowledge in each specialized field has made this especially true. As a firm grows, staff growth poses difficulties in communication. To meet these, the firm must radically change its mode of operation to accommodate the injection of additional staff. Otherwise there is a tendency toward heavy centralization and little action down the line. Staff may actually retard the growth and development of lower-level management.

Sometimes it seems difficult to get uniform procedures throughout the company, and policies are applied differently in different areas. The need for a staff function is therefore suggested to the chief executive. When he sets up the staff function, however, he in effect places an additional limit on the line. He naturally expects the staff job to produce value and this means some interjection into the work of the line. This interjection must be recognized as normal.

One added comment in regard to the growth of staff: It is a common fallacy to feel that the proportion of indirect help to direct is a good measurement of company effectiveness. ("After all, these indirect people do not really produce.") In actual practice, this tends to be less and less true. Generally, the more modern a firm is in its operation the higher is the proportion of staff people to line people. You can readily see why this is true. The firm is capitalizing on the various sciences that may be available. Results achieved by adding additional staff usually mean a reduction in number of line people needed. Sometimes a firm may be very proud of the fact that it has not increased the number of its indirect people. Such a company may not move ahead as fast as its competition and cannot understand why. The reason may well be that it is not using skilled staff where it is needed. New developments tend to pass such a company by. Budgets may work in this direction. They may inhibit the needed expansion of staff by discouraging the additional expense. It is usually easier to get approval of additional line expense.

Automation generally requires more staff in relationship to line. More skilled specialists are needed as against straight operators. Service functions become more critical than operating functions. A subtle change in thinking is required in the management approach of a firm as it becomes more and more modern and takes on more automated methods.

What are the special problems that develop when a firm starts adding staff functions? Staff should help the line do its work better. However, staff and line are frequently in conflict as to what should be done. Staff may argue that its people cannot get full accomplishment because line does not cooperate with them. Line, in turn, feels that staff is somewhat impractical in its procedures. Some firms experience a constantly increasing cost of staff activities, finally reaching a point where an executive doubts whether he is getting a worthwhile return out of this tremendous accretion. Sometimes, with this growth of staff, line begins to shirk its responsibility, saying, "That's the staff's responsibility." Staff, in turn, tries to run the operation (without really being accountable for its success).

Autonomous vs. *Manipulative Staffs*

It may help to consider the characteristics of some typical staff operations. Line people often feel that staff interferes with their operation; that staff wants to do everything. This complaint is usually directed against the type of staff which we would consider "manipulative"—staff people who give advice on actual day-to-day operations. "Autonomous" staffs, on the other hand, can generally do their work somewhat independently of the flow of work of the line. They do not seem to interfere as much with the regular work of the line. A legal function may operate this way. In personnel an employee-recruiting function can be a somewhat autonomous staff function, one which does not impinge heavily on the day-to-day operations of the line. When the personnel function gets into salary and management-bonus administration, however, it tends to be manipulative. These activities get into the basic relationship between a supervisor and his subordinate. It is this type of staff work that breeds the greatest conflicts.

How can you reduce the problem of manipulative staffs and still get accomplishment? Once this manipulative-versus-autonomous aspect is recognized, the manipulative job can often be designed so that it gradually becomes more autonomous. One way to achieve this is by a careful definition of the limits of the staff area, reducing the possibility of conflict. Limits should be very carefully set so that staff has a distinct sphere within which it may operate and contribute. The more this can be done, the more the manipulative staff tends to approach the autonomous type, and the less disharmony with the line develops.

The Control Staff

There is another type of staff that is set up primarily for advice on trends. These are "control" staffs. They should not advise on **what** should be done. It is their job merely to point out deviations to various management people so that they can take action. Cost-recording functions tend to fall in this area. Quality-control–record functions and sales-statistical functions are usually of this type.

The real danger is that the control staff may start to give advice as to what should be done instead of interpreting all the data they have at their command so that the individual on the job can more effectively make a decision himself. This interpretive function should usually be the main purpose of the control staff. The job setup that is most effective, therefore, is one where the control staff is held specifically responsible for providing records and interpretations that result in action, but **not** for making suggestions as to what action should be taken. The staff man is then encouraged to interpret realistically but he is kept from, in effect, supervising the line. At the same time he is measured by the action taken. He is therefore much more likely to critically review the applicability and the voluminousness of his records.

The "Assistant-to" Type of Staff

A special type of staff job is the so-called "Assistant-to" position. The position seems logical to a busy executive who has a great many details to check up on. It comes into prominence as a firm grows larger and a chief becomes inaccessible. Frequently it can be eliminated by better delegation from the superior.

The basic function of the Assistant-to is to extend the scope of his superior by interpreting to others down the line what the superior's stand or opinion probably would be on a particular problem and, in turn, to feed information upward to the superior. If the Assistant-to is close to all the problems and thinking of his superior, he can very often aid in giving guidance to subordinates of his superior by interpreting what the superior would probably think on a particular subject.

In setting up such a position, however, great care must be taken to define the job so it is not that of an "assistant." In other words, such a job should carry no authority to give orders. Any subordinate should have the right to go around the Assistant-to to inquire of the superior as to what his opinion or suggestion might be. The Assistant-to is primarily responsible, then, for greasing the wheels of action by providing accurate interpretations of the thinking of the superior, even though the superior is not there. To the extent that these interpretations are inaccurate, the Assistant-to is a liability. One danger is that he may give his own personal interpretations in offering suggestions to the subordinates of his superior. When he does this, he tends to get into trouble, and frequently harms rather than helps the operation. Or he may give directions to others, seeming to supervise them. Resentment can develop and, in effect, a two-boss setup. The other subordinates of the superior may begin to report to the Assistant-to. He may, also, come to be looked on as a kind of Gestapo or ambitious climber.

An Assistant-to position may be regarded as a training ground for future executives. In our opinion it should not be set up for that purpose if it is not needed. It is apt to become a "crown prince" job, and a good man may actually be spoiled rather than helped by being placed in it. It may be difficult to hold him accountable—the best way to make a man develop.

HOW SHOULD STAFF BE SET UP?

Unfortunately, it is all too easy to develop a large staff group that is not contributing to the success of the firm. Sometimes an executive feels that a staff group is growing without limit, and yet finds the expansion difficult to check. At the same time that staff is increasing, it seems to cost twice as much to carry through on projects that formerly appeared quite simple. These developments often stem from a poor approach to the initial establishment of staff functions.

Staff Must Be Needed

A common error is to set up staff simply because other good firms have done so. The executive feels that he too wants to be modern—a poor basis for adding any staff function. It may turn out to be of little value to his firm. At times firms set up a staff function merely as a training device. Such a setup usually leads to excessive staff and often to a training job that lacks accountability, so that even as a training device it may be poor. Fundamentally *there must be a need for the staff.*

The executive may be well advised, in considering a staff function, to first ask this question: "What is the result that needs to be obtained?" Then: "What type of staff can accomplish this result best and at what cost?" It is surprising how much more effective an executive will be in getting a perspective on needed staff functions.

Can the Line Do the Work?

When an executive faces a difficult problem it seems logical to set up a man (a staff man) to concentrate on it. However, the executive should ask this further question: "Could the line possibly do the work reasonably well?" I emphasize here "reasonably well." Staff, you recall, must get its results through someone else. It is basically a "second-class" way of doing anything. In addition, it means added cost. First the executive should try to devise some way whereby the line could do the work at least reasonably well. It is amazing how frequently this approach can eliminate proposed but unneeded staff functions.

For example, in many plants a foreman can handle inspection problems adequately if accountability is set up properly. If this is possible, it eliminates a second party, an inspector supervisor. In sales departments special promotion work can often be carried out by the salesman in the territory if the job is properly designed. He can be made to feel a strong sense of accountability for accomplishment. He has to live with it. It is, of course, obvious that if you can get the line to take the responsibility and do the job, it is much easier to check excessive staff growth. It is also easier to maintain accountability—always the key to sound administration.

Is the Work Specialized?

Another check on the need for staff is whether or not the staff position proposed requires a specialized ability. Ordinarily staff functions should not be set up on activities that are relatively easy to learn. The line is usually a more direct way to accomplishment. An executive or a manager is well advised to spot these simple functions and see whether he can eliminate the need for staff. As a rule of thumb, whenever a staff function requires relatively little specialized knowledge, he should seriously question whether there is not a way to get the line to do it.

A typical example of a simple function might be certain machine-scheduling work, which can often be carried out effectively by a foreman. A first-line supervisor in any department can do simple methods work if you set up the right kind of accountability and authority for him, providing he does not exceed his span of control.

Although specialized knowledge may be necessary when setting up certain functions, their actual administration can often be handled by people without specialized knowledge. Staff functions that fit this category should probably be limited to the initial setup and the over-all audit of the broad procedure. The actual administration should be handled by line people. If this can be done, you usually get a much more effective operation.

A typical example is salary administration. Frequently salary administrators go too far—to the point where they are practically dictating individual salary increases. Within sound and well-explained policy, the supervisor, if he is properly accountable, should be the one to control increases, capitalizing on the raise system in stimulating his employees to sound operation.

Do You Need Over-all Control?

A staff function may be needed where a uniform over-all policy is required, one that crosses departmental lines either to get people to work together or to prevent the occurrence of difficult precedents which may affect future action. Some coordinating function must be established that supersedes the authority of individual departments and helps them understand the interdepartmental problems. Typical examples of these might be personnel functions, over-all accounting functions, or legal functions. However, we should point out one important principle in the approach to these functions. The executive should carefully weigh which part of them requires uniform policy and which part can be subject to a certain amount of local determination. Often much less over-all control is needed than is at first assumed. Executives frequently make the error of setting up staff to cover a whole function, because part of it does require uniform application throughout all departments. As the company grows, problems that occur between central staff and local staff can be traced to this error. There is usually a distinct limit to the over-all company-wide control that is needed—it should be highlighted when setting up the staff.

Planning vs. *Doing*

Staff is usually effective for a planning function as opposed to a "doing" function—usually the line's work. Whenever staff is "doing" you might question whether this work should be a separate staff function. "Doing" actively impinges on the line—it is very likely that the line could do the work better. The danger point in staff planning is usually reached when the line is not allowed adequate authority leeway to accomplish its objectives, when staff is practically controlling "doing." In a large firm this is usually evidenced by an excessive number of procedure manuals. It may be quite a project to find the correct page and paragraph that applies to a given problem.

Test by Double the Cost

Too frequently a staff function is not accountable for its true cost of operation. As a working rule, we have found the following approach helpful in making sure that staff is worth the "chips." Since the staff function by its very definition must accomplish a result through someone else, this usually means that another person must also contribute to it. As a working rule a 50-50 split in credit is often realistic. In other words, if a staff function might effect a saving of $40,000, usually $20,000 of this depends on the degree to which the line people put their all into the problem. It is also important to consider the fact that any person on the payroll usually costs you much more than his base salary. Most office people cost about double their base salary when you add the cost of fringe benefits, leave, supervision, supplies, etc. If, therefore, you feel that a staff job could save $40,000 a year, you would start out by cutting this in half, since line people are probably contributing substantially to this result. The staff man would then be viewed as personally contributing $20,000. Since the man must contribute twice his salary (to pay for fringe benefits, leave, supervision, supplies, etc.) simply to pay his way, the firm should probably not pay him more than $10,000 base salary a year to accomplish this $40,000 saving if it is not to end up with a net loss on the function. Obviously, this rule-of-thumb approach cannot be applied specifically in every case. It is often of considerable help, however, in analyzing the advisability of either developing or retaining a staff operation.

Staff should be looked at as an added cost. It must produce value over and above its cost, including the time of the line that it appropriates. A staff man is placed in an untenable position when the potential value of his work will not pay for itself. Inevitably the line senses this fact and opposition develops.

Many times a staff man may initially pay for himself for a couple of years. After the major work has been done, however, there may be less need for the function, and it should be eliminated or curtailed. The cost approach described above is often helpful in controlling the growth of staff functions. It is also especially helpful in planning special projects for staff. Sometimes apparently tempting projects just will not pay for the added cost of the staff work required.

Is There a Continuing Need?

There is a tendency for a staff function to perpetuate itself once it is set up. It is natural for the staff man to want to feel that he is still needed. Management, in turn, quite naturally tends to recall past contributions of the staff and so justify it even though there may be little present value coming from its work. In our opinion, staff functions should be reviewed every six months or every year to ascertain that the function, in total or in part, is still necessary. The point made in the paragraph above is especially helpful in making such an analysis. Test staff's present-day contributions against four times the staff salary cost. You often find that functions that once paid off are no longer paying their way.

For example, an expediter may have been very effective at a period of tight timing requirements or material shortages. Conditions have changed, however, and he may no longer contribute in proportion to his cost. The same may be true of a cost control man who was very effective in getting all line people to be very cost-conscious. At a certain point in the game, the value of continuing the job as originally set up may be questioned.

This point is especially apropos when you differentiate between the establishment of a staff function and its continuance. In the case of most functions, the cost in time required for installation is much greater than that for maintenance. When you put in a new function, you ordinarily build up personnel to accommodate the installation phases. After the function is operating well, there is normally a tendency to retain the same initial staff. Ambitious staff men try to find things to do. Excuses are given as to why the full staff is still necessary. We have observed empirically that in many staff functions the installation phase requires roughly double the personnel that is needed to continue it. Obviously, this rule cannot be applied perfectly in every case, but it too is helpful as a starting point in analyzing the number of people needed for continuing staff functions.

GEAR STAFF TO RESULTS

We have maintained throughout this book that it is fundamental to the design of any job that you state the results you expect from it. This rule also applies to staff jobs. *Staff, too, must be responsible for results.* In many firms problems of staff functions begin with the fact that the results staff is expected to accomplish have not been defined. The comment is often made, "Staff is not accountable for results. They are there simply to advise and consult with the line." In our opinion this probably means that the executive has not fully established the need for staff in the first place; otherwise he would have clearly defined the results he expects. Every job should have a contribution to make toward the objectives of the enterprise.

Staff on Results, Not Activity

There are several important reasons for insisting that staff produce results. Without a definition of results expected, staff can never be held truly accountable. A flexible standard tends to exist. Staff members will be held accountable by activity, which is subject to many interpretations. There is then a tendency for the staff function to grow without limit. In staff's "advisory" position it is natural for it to emphasize activity, although the activity may not be harmonious with the results the line is trying to get. Line may then feel that staff is not working with them but in another direction, causing problems between the staff and the line. Staff may be busy with one project after another; in many cases, however, it is highly questionable whether the projects are helping secure better operation. In addition, staff tends to continue long after it is needed; it is extremely difficult to eliminate a staff function when you have not defined the results expected of it—the activity it engages in always seems so logical.

Staff problems are accentuated when staff becomes entrenched and focuses on activity instead of results. Staff people tend to go off on tangents. They do not seem to have time to do the specific work that the line requires, and yet they may not seem to accomplish much. Staff may be actively promoting the "professionalism" of its field (or its status) instead of the contribution it should be making to the success of the enterprise.

There is a critical point to be emphasized concerning

the relationship of the responsibilities of line and staff. Line has a job to do. Staff is supposed to help it do this job better. *From the point of view of results, staff and line always overlap.* It is implicit in the definition of staff that this is true. Staff is merely trying to expedite results that the line is held accountable for—though, of course, only part of the results that the line is held accountable for. Here too the application of the theory of unique accountability can be the source of a poor organization setup. The results expected of staff should be part of the results that line is attempting to get.

There is a need for an extremely clear-cut definition of the area in which the staff results are to be achieved, however. Conscientious staff often assumes that almost any activity is within its province. A militant staff man may appear to take over, so that line feels that staff is running the whole show. Line becomes confused in trying to decide what should be discussed with staff and what should not. Line, then, either tends to give up or to oppose staff.

A further point in defining results for staff: If possible, *line and staff jobs should be separate.* When a man has specific line responsibilities to supervise other line people, it is difficult for him to give good staff service. When the pressure is on him to produce, there is a natural tendency for him to favor his own line department. Even if he does not do this, the other line people are still inclined to feel that he does. It is generally much more satisfactory organization design to combine various staff functions rather than to combine staff with line. In some cases different combinations of staff work evolve than you might first anticipate. Applying this rule may be a particular problem in small companies or in branches; in some cases it may have to be violated until the firm or branch grows larger.

Keep Staff Results Harmonious with the Line

It often appears that staff and line are working in different directions. Perhaps the line thinks staff is impractical. Staff sometimes tries to force inapplicable procedures on the line. The line people then refuse to accept ideas from staff. The situation causes frustration in the staff man, who is only partially successful.

When staff is responsible for "consulting with," "advising," etc., it is usually accountable for activity. As we have pointed out earlier, activity is subject to many interpretations. It is therefore very easy under such a setup for staff work to be out of harmony with the line, and staff-line conflict develops. To minimize this conflict *the results expected of staff should be harmonious with those expected of the line.* A very careful analysis is required. One of the most prevalent violations of this rule occurs in the plant where quality people are frequently held accountable for maintaining a high level of quality but are not accountable for cost or for waste. It is only natural for an aggressive quality man to set very high quality requirements so that he is sure to be in the clear. At the same time, however, his action causes very high waste and high manufacturing cost. In essence, he has superimposed a heavy burden, for which he is not accountable, on the line. The situation has developed because the results expected of him are not fully harmonious with those of the line. He should probably be accountable for a level of quality and for the negative effect of increasing waste. He must then balance the waste increase against the extra quality obtained.

The same thing can be true in other departments. A staff product sales manager may put a great deal of pressure on salesmen to push particular types of accounts. The salesman, however, is acountable for a specified volume. If he puts in the effort on certain accounts expected by the product sales manager, he will not reach the over-all volume expected of him. In essence, then, these two men are opposed to each other, because the results one is trying to get are not really harmonious with those of the other.

Be Watchful of the Project

Defining harmonious staff results may be difficult in the case of certain technical men. In order to get flexibility it seems natural to the technical supervisor to define the results expected of his men by project. He can then use them wherever he has problems. Project responsibility can be a source of conflict between staff and line. When a staff man is accountable for a specific project only, he may actually be accountable for results that are not harmonious with those expected of the line.

A common illustration of this difficulty is the case of the methods engineer who is accountable only by specific project. He may impose a procedure on the line that will make his project look good but will be extremely costly in its effect on other work. For example, suppose that he develops a fine project that sets up a new procedure for certain work. From his studies he indicates an expected saving of $50,000. When the line supervisor follows this procedure, however, he finds that he increases his problems in getting other work done. He, therefore, loses most of the $50,000 that the methods engineer presumably saved. People tend to point the finger at him for not accomplishing his results, while the methods engineer is complimented for his wonderful project. In essence, however, the results that the methods engineer achieved and is complimented for were not really harmonious with those expected of the line. Antagonism develops between the methods engineer and the line supervision.

A chief industrial engineer often feels he has more flexibility when holding his men accountable by project. The losses, however, may overshadow the gains that would be realized if responsibility were defined by the department served. In addition, the latter approach tends to develop more responsibility in the engineer for training the line people to do much of the simpler methods work themselves, and much greater gains result.

The problem may occur in a little different way in an over-all product development department. Perhaps new product design is laid out on a project basis. A long list of projects is presented, but the basic accountability for improvement of the product line itself is not stated. The project list seems perfectly logical because in this way you can put specialists on particular problems. Considerable work may have been done, but since no over-all accountability for the product line has been developed, gaps and weak points develop in the product line which are more serious than the gains made in the particular projects. These, however, are not the concern of the chief of product development. He is busy pushing the long list of projects to be completed. Some key designs needed for the line, however, never appear on this list or else appear at the bottom, to be done if he has time.

SOUND AUTHORITY FOR STAFF

We mentioned earlier that there is a tendency for militant staff to run the whole show. Line may feel, then, that staff is trying to take over without being accountable. A conscientious staff man feels justified in demanding that line comply with his recommendations. After all, isn't he the expert in the field? Line is not, however, particularly receptive to the new ideas proposed by staff. How can an executive resolve this basic authority conflict?

A popular concept regards staff as entirely a service function, one which should carry no authority whatsoever, except perhaps the "authority of ideas." The viewpoint stems naturally from the idea that only line should be accountable for results. In our opinion this is merely sidestepping the issue; it is giving up on organization definition. It has been our observation that those staff services that make valuable contributions are, in effect, assuming a certain kind of authority, which is recognized and accepted by the line.

Definition of Staff Authority

What authority should staff have? Let us assume that you have followed the suggestions proposed earlier in this chapter. First, you have made sure that the staff is needed

—that there is a requirement for it, that it has a niche to fill. Second, and related to this, its work is specialized or has interdepartmental implications so that it is questionable whether line could do the work effectively. Third, you have made staff accountable for results, and results that are harmonious with those expected of the line—they are both pointed in the same direction. In addition, the sphere of staff has been carefully delineated. Under these circumstances, we would suggest that staff have the following authority:

> *Within its own limited field the word of the staff man holds unless proven wrong by the line.*

You can see then that on decisions in its own field staff would take precedence over line. What we are really saying is that the expert decides on the action. You probably see some negative implications of this approach. But remember: First you need to define the results which justify staff. There must be a need for an expert. Under this concept staff men must not be juniors, as is so often the case. Instead they must frequently be more experienced than the men of the line, at least in the particular area of their specialty. (Acceptance of this concept may require a change of present practice in the manning of staff positions.)

You may feel that this approach straps the line. Actually, they should have the right of appeal. If line disagrees with what staff wants to do and cannot convince staff, they may go to someone higher up to get the staff recommendation reversed. In practice, they would not have to do this very frequently because of one cardinal point! Remember, the staff is now fully accountable for the results of their action.

They are accountable on some of the same results expected of the line. They soon recognize that they need the line's help to make staff ideas work. Staff is measured not by an appraisal of a plan per se but purely by the results of the installation of the plan. Under those circumstances, they hesitate to be too autocratic and dictate to the line when the line feels an idea is not going to work. They are now much more inclined to solicit line's help and advice.

For example, a merchandiser is quite careful about ignoring the comment of sales managers when a measurement of his results is the number of sales achieved. The production control man is not nearly so dictatorial with foremen and superintendents when the extra cost resulting from his scheduling counts against him as well as against supervision. He is much more inclined to get the advice of line and discuss a problem carefully with them to make sure that he is coming to the best conclusion. On the other hand, under these circumstances line is much more willing to accept the decisions of the staff. Staff is accountable just as they are.

Staff Must Go Direct

Staff is often handicapped because line supervisors do not carry through on their suggestions. Staff works out fine plans and presents them to a manager, but they never seem to come into effect. It is hard to get action through right down to the bottom level where the work is done. Staff is likely to have this difficulty when they are not allowed to go direct but must go through channels.

If you want staff to be most effective, you should create

a setup that permits them to go directly to any member of management who is expected to put their suggestions into effect. In other words, you should have an organization design that eliminates red tape. You may ask, "Doesn't this procedure go around supervision?" Perhaps, to some extent. But supervision should OK the basic setup. *It should be the obligation of every supervisor at every level to approve a working arrangement between his subordinates and staff, so that staff may go direct within this arrangement.* Keep in mind, too, that we are talking about staff functions that are going to be accountable for results that actually help the line. Under these circumstances, you will usually find that supervision is willing to allow the staff to go direct to subordinates in order to achieve its accomplishment. Supervision saves time by the procedure.

Staff as a Line Restriction

As a company sets up staff services, line often becomes "fed up" with staff. They feel that staff is holding them back; that they (line) do not have the authority they used to have before all these staff people were inflicted on them. They point this up as a sound reason why the firm should avoid staff and go back to the old days of the simple straight-line organization.

As his firm grows to the point of taking on staff, it is very important that an executive recognize that efficient use of staff involves a different mode of operation—that staff is a restriction on the line. In effect, setting up a staff function imposes a policy limitation on supervision wherever the staff impinges. It actually reduces the authority of the line, and there should be no doubt about this. But remember, if the staff service is necessary and helpful, its effect is to enhance the effectiveness of every member of supervision. Its need must, however, be constantly reviewed.

A common argument is that the use of staff destroys the unity of command. Line no longer feels that they have control—staff seems to give all the orders to the men. This situation should ordinarily not exist. Staff has a limited sphere within which it works, and supervisors should know exactly what this sphere is and how staff operates. But the fact that staff must be recognized as a policy limitation on the line is inescapable.

If a firm is to get full value from automation, this limiting factor involved in the use of staff must be clearly understood. With an increase in mechanization, staff must usually have more authority, since the expert now has a greater and more critical effect. A finer and finer definition of the area of decision and sphere of influence of each individual expert is required. It cannot be avoided. You must recognize, however, that the net effect is to impose a further restriction on certain supervisory personnel. In addition, lower-level supervisory jobs will tend to resemble those of higher managers in their mode of operation, including staff subordinates.

16

Minimize Staff-Line Opposition

A STAFF MAN is usually directed to analyze a particular problem and develop solutions. Beyond this the setup is often vague. If things work out well, the staff man naturally takes the credit. If not, he can almost always see where the line failed by not following through on his recommendations. The line then becomes opposed to staff. They also may feel that staff is trying to foist cumbersome operations on them through some "crackbrain" ivory-tower plan. Under these circumstances staff has difficulty getting line to carry out their ideas, so they become frustrated and blame line for not being open-minded.

Hold Staff Accountable for Results

The key point is that after you have defined results expected of staff, they must be accountable by results. If they are not, they tend to glorify their function out of proportion to its value and focus on the special activities common to their field, whether these aid the line or not.

Some firms hold staff accountable only for what they call "technical adequacy." What is the effect? Staff develops a great pride in its "modern" procedures (and usually in all of them). The sense of professionalism that so often causes the man to deviate from true accomplishment is intensified. Staff tends to be more rigid in holding to "accepted" procedures of the field, pointing out that many other companies use them. By this fact staff presumably "proves" that they are right.

Personnel men who apply all the "accepted" techniques but do little to check their effect on employee effectiveness exemplify this type of staff, as do engineers who quote engineering society codes or broad surveys or statements regarding their function instead of focusing on their net effect on operations. An attorney joins this group if he always gives you a complete legal opinion indicating conclusively why you cannot take action but does little to show you how you can move at a reasonable risk.

The staff man must be accountable for results if you wish to control the growth of staff. A staff octopus develops when there is no accountability for accomplishment that helps the line—accomplishment as balanced against cost. A staff man becomes more hesitant about asking for an extension of his service when he knows that he is going to be accountable both for the results and for the cost of his service.

Making a staff man accountable for results also tends to minimize the flood of reports that often flow up the line.

When staff people continually circulate reports on what they are doing, it is usually a symptom that they are accountable by activity (not by results).

It is perfectly natural for the staff man to do this. He is then relieved of accountability. He notified everyone! Since such reporting goes to the top, it tends to show up the line people and is unlikely to increase staff-line cooperation. In addition, these reports can prove a burden to executives up the line in trying to separate the wheat from the chaff.

Double Accountability Is Necessary

Frequently the reason line feels staff is not on their side, is not cooperative, or tends to work in the wrong direction, is that staff is not accountable in the same way as line. This feeling is especially common where people hold to the philosophy that only the line is accountable for results. Since the staff is not accountable for results, they may, as we said above, easily work on activities that aim in a different direction from the results expected of the line.

This leads to a fundamental principle for the accountability of staff—the principle of double credit. It is simply that:

> *Both staff and line should get full credit for any accomplishment of either the staff or the line in the area that the staff is set up to cover.*

Even though staff may do very little to help the line accomplish a particular result, it will get full credit. On the other hand, if the line man has done very little to help the staff idea work, he still gets the full credit. (Usually neither of these extremes is typical.) They both get full credit.

This rule may go against the grain for some executives. However, its application will encourage a much greater accomplishment from both staff and line. They will be encouraged to work together because it is to each one's advantage. They are both accountable and will get credit only when the result expected is achieved. It is unrealistic to hope that the staff man should be happy in the knowledge that he can make some slight contribution to the line even though he gets no credit for it. It is hard to get a creative staff man with initiative to assume this spineless, self-effacing role. On the other side, it is certainly also unrealistic to assume that the line man will enjoy having the staff man fussing around in his activity unless he feels that if something works, he, the line man, will also get full credit. You can see that here we recognize a complete overlap in accountability. In staff areas there is never unique accountability. It is staff's function to help the line do its job better. A line man must always be accountable for his total operation, including the parts where staff helps. A result expected of a staff man is only one of the results expected of a line man.

The principle of the dual accountability of staff and line is an extremely important point for an executive to consider when setting up staff and line functions. The concept should be strongly reflected in such areas as pay, promotion, and performance appraisal—all of which influence accountability. It should be part of the basic design of the job, if the job setup is to encourage both staff and line to work together effectively toward sound over-all results.

The Principle of Negative Result

In Chapter 4, page 36, we stated that it was generally advisable to hold a man accountable for the negative effect of overdiligence in achieving a result. There is usually an optimum point beyond which a result may add little, or may actually be negative, since imbalance tends to develop. This principle is especially applicable to staff jobs. For example, staff may not be concerned with cost. They may push otherwise desirable activities to the point where the cost becomes excessive. A sincere but "narrow specialist" may have a shortsighted perspective of his place in the total operation. He may push his specialty to the point where it interferes with operation. It is especially helpful in steering staff in the right direction to make them accountable for both the negative and the positive result of their actions.

For example, a credit manager should often be accountable for both the cost of credit (losses plus administration) and also for the loss in sales resulting from tight credit restrictions. If he is too tight, he gets hit by loss of orders. If he is too loose, his financial losses rise. Accountability forces him to blend these two considerations. It is to his advantage to do so.

This approach is particularly valuable in regard to record functions. Record functions are frequently able to make a showing by pointing up all the deficiencies of employees to executives. This has a negative effect on the stimulation of supervision down the line, who may feel that their authority is restricted and become overly cautious. The record people are usually not accountable for this negative effect. A conscientious record man may become overly diligent about pointing out errors (often minor errors) because he is never accountable for the negative effect of his finger pointing. He may become isolated; others tend to resent him because he is not working with the over-all team.

The "optimum principle" of results is especially applicable to staff people. Trained staff men quite naturally tend to glorify their own activity. They frequently highlight the procedures of their fields rather than the achievement of results. If, however, you can hold them accountable for each result on an optimum basis, you are better able to secure sound contribution from them. The executive must carefully determine for each staff result the point beyond which the result ceases to be a net addition to company results—the optimum point. It should be part of his organization planning. One reason staff should report at as low a level as possible in the line hierarchy, as we shall see later, is that the superior will be much closer to these problems and be able to do this planning more realistically. The staff man actually gains because the setup reduces the possibility of friction with the line people.

Tie in the Record System to Accountability

One weakness of record systems in many companies is that they do not apply to staff operations. Considering that staff is usually held accountable merely for advising or consulting with the line, this is understandable. As a consequence, staff does not really know how well it is doing in its accomplishment of results. Since it is hard to tell whether staff is paying off, staff may be retained merely because other companies have it—"It must be good practice." Such a situation is actually unfair to a good staff man and to the firm wishing to get value from him.

If the rule of double credit for staff and line is to be effective, the record system must reflect this double credit. There must be a double charge to staff and line for the same result. The charge is usually included in the record of the over-all result that line is trying to get. In addition, there should also be a side record of the accomplishment of the results in the staff area in order to sharpen the staff operation.

For example, there should be some record that indicates the net results a safety engineer is getting in a plant. The data on plant safety experience could be a good measurement. Records should be kept showing the results a market research man is getting in his studies. These may be only spot checks of sales accomplishment in the area he affects, but they are better than none, especially at the start. If you do not keep records of employment activities, it is going to be difficult to hold the employment function accountable for those results it is supposed to achieve to help the line. Perhaps records of the productivity of new hires versus previous hires, new employee turnover, and number of referrals to line per placement could be used. The principle applies to almost any kind of staff activity. As a rule of thumb: When you have a staff function of which it seems impossible to keep a record, the staff function may very well have no real contribution to make.

BROADEN THE SUPERVISION TO INCLUDE STAFF

Staff may have difficulty blending in with line because proper weight has not been given to the type of supervision required to make staff most effective. There are often more problems in supervising staff people than there are with those of the line. It frequently takes careful thinking through to set up staff results so that they are harmonious with line results. In addition, there must be careful check and follow-up to be certain that the staff work is effective. The supervisor must also give staff supervisory backing and encourage other line people to aid the staff man. Many times conflicts occur between staff and line because this broader supervisory requirement has not been recognized. Staff people usually need more supervision than line people do.

Span of Control—Number of Relationships

By its very operation, staff incurs many critical relationships with other people. Staff does not generally accomplish anything except through the line. Relationships of subordinates require time on the part of the manager to smooth over. And it is his job to smooth them over! Since staff has many relationships, a manager of staff functions cannot usually supervise as many people as he could if he had only line people under him. Many companies assume that a manager can easily take on the supervision of staff functions in addition to all the line functions he supervised before. This is not true. In such a case politics and lack of cooperation often occur because a manager has actually exceeded his span of control. He has not recognized that one of the jobs of any manager is to smooth over the relationships between his subordinates, and that this takes time.

Have Staff Report down the Line

Staff people naturally wish to report as high as possible in the organization echelon. It is easier then to build up their departments. Also, everyone likes to report to top brass if he can. Paradoxically, they are usually less effective there—staff may be too removed from the problems they are trying to solve. Wherever you can break up a staff department and have a staff man report directly to the line manager he helps, he tends to be more effective. It is usually wise to *have your staff people report to the lowest level possible.*

A sales service man, for example, may always work in the Eastern territory. It might be most effective to have him report directly to the Eastern Division sales manager. A methods engineer may always be working in the tooling department. Under those circumstances he may be most effective reporting directly to the superintendent of tooling, rather than to a chief methods engineer who in turn reports to the plant manager. The line then feels that the staff man is on their team and that they have more control over his work. They therefore become better sold on him.

The staff man is tied much more closely to the results of the area in which he is working. He is inclined to develop more sympathy for the problems of the line. The setup is also a fine experience for a superintendent. Since he learns to be a manager of staff functions, he is much better equipped to advance to the position, say, of plant manager. The staff man, in turn, learns early in his career that he must help line. His boss is the superintendent!

You may argue that a chief methods engineer could give a methods engineer closer technical supervision. Probably, but the other advantages often outweigh the disadvantages, particularly since a reasonable functional relationship can usually be developed between the methods engineer and the chief methods engineer.

Train Supervisors to Use Staff

Because of the staff setup, supervisors often do not learn how to use staff, and when they are promoted they have some difficulty coordinating staff people. The problem stems from the fact that the results expected of staff and line have not been blended and accountability forced accordingly. Supervisors must learn to accept and use new staff as part of their responsibility. New sciences must be assimilated, but they must be assimilated in the course of the regular operation! Directives do not accomplish this. A management climate must be developed to encourage the acceptance of staff.

Responsibility must be imposed on supervision up the line to guide and train the supervisors below them in accepting staff functions, to explain the need for staff, to review staff objectives, and to smooth over relationships with staff. Planning is required to ensure that staff and line have mutual objectives. Fundamentally, it should be the job of the manager up the line to pave the way and educate his subordinates on the profitable use of staff. Part of this preparation for staff includes a careful analysis of the results to be achieved, so that the results expected of a new staff function are harmonious with those expected of the line supervisors.

Completed Function for Staff

Staff often spends too much time on a project. They may want to philosophize on all the alternative possibilities and are slow in making a decision. They may often come to their chief to discuss a problem that is half-baked. In doing this they develop "interesting" problems to discuss in a "preliminary" way, but they impose on the chief the burden of thinking through, probably on inadequate facts. One of the essentials in supervising staff functions is that staff be required to carry through on the rule of completed function discussed in Chapter 2. In other words, we are asking a staff man to provide answers, not questions. He should be encouraged to stick his neck out with recommendations even if the decision is beyond his authority, as it probably would be. If it is within his authority, why bother the chief at all? Staff becomes truly accountable and a stronger help to the line in accomplishing results.

Staff people too often waste a great deal of time in discussions with the line people. This tendency must be curbed. It is their job to help the line, not to waste its time. One effective step in this direction is to keep records of all the line time spent with the staff man and charge it against his projects. He is then forced to be accountable for all the time of other people that he wastes. Sometimes such a record is difficult to keep up, but even a spot check may be effective in driving the problem home to the staff man. Often he has not realized the amount of line time that he takes. With some engineering and personnel functions this procedure can be a valuable supervisory tool for highlighting some of the hidden costs of staff work that are often not recognized.

17

Expansion into Multiple Organization

WHILE THE PROBLEM of integrating staff with line is similar under all conditions, there are some special ramifications in coordinating staff with line when the enterprise becomes complex. The problems are variable, but they must be solved to fit into over-all objectives. With increased complexity it becomes difficult to get uniform approaches on different work. The very elaborateness of the organization structure frequently makes it difficult to carefully think through the role of staff. Staff and line conflicts increase, or staff grows excessively because it is now much harder to clearly fix staff accountability. There is therefore a greater tendency to rely on activity, with a consequent overemphasis on manuals, instruction booklets, and procedure sheets. These in turn tend to retard individual initiative down the line—a supervisor never knows when he may be violating some procedure. Engaging in company politics appears more advantageous to an individual than aggressive grappling with difficult problems, even to individuals at the higher levels.

Combine by Results

Because a program has many ramifications in multiple organization, parts of it are assigned to different people, usually on the basis of specialized activity. Since the parts overlap when viewed from the standpoint of results, many people may impinge on a problem. The line becomes confused as to whom they should follow. In addition, the staff specialist tries to develop a ring of sanctity around his particular area in order to maintain control of his function. No one else should touch it! It becomes all the more important here to clarify the final result that staff is trying to get.

One effective way to meet the problem is to *combine those staff functions that work toward one result.* At a lower level, particularly, several of these staff activities might be handled by one man. The number of contacts that line must endure are thus reduced and less coordination is required of the line manager. Relationships are simplified. While the staff man is not quite as expert in each speciality as if he handled only one, his total contribution to the enterprise is often greater because it is easier, with fewer people, to establish accountability.

Without an effort to make these combinations, the work toward a result may go back and forth between groups and finally gets lost in the shuffle. Or so much attention is given to individual activities that the end result becomes confused. This zigzag flow of work eventually winds up with excessive cost, poor communications, many coordinating meetings, and poor timing of the final result.

An outstanding example of this confusion often occurs in the area of product development. Many people may have a hand in one or more segments of the problem. It is difficult to coordinate all these segments. Each one tends to be a bottleneck. In addition, gaps occur between activities of individuals, with no one assuming responsibility for them. As a consequence, new products tend to lag, fail to meet deadlines, or are too costly.

One good way to approach this situation is to check the responsibility flow of the work. List each small step that must be accomplished and, next to it, who must accomplish it. The listing often offers insight for determining the limits of the contribution that a particular staff should make, suggests combinations that may be made, and makes sure that no link in the accomplishment chain is missed.

Following this principle, personnel and hourly incentive functions, for instance, may be combined, since employee relations and union problems will affect incentive results, while incentive installations, in turn, could lead to very undesirable contract clauses. Both groups should be aiming at the same thing, more effective employee effort.

Separate Long-range from Short-range Planning

One of the most troublesome problems for a growth company particularly is that of getting the long-range planning work done without interfering with short-range achievement. The importance of integrating sound long-range planning is intensified when you get into complex enterprises. Many times long-range projects are very costly, particularly when high capital expenditure and complex integrating problems are involved. Crises seem to arise that always justify quick, expedient decisions; there is a tendency to focus on "hot" problems. At other times long-range effort is carried on at the sacrifice of short-range endeavor. Everything seems to be viewed as a long-range problem and current operations suffer.

As soon as a company has reached the size where it is economically possible, it is generally wise to *separate long-range planning from short-range results* in almost any area. For example, if there is a considerable amount of long-range engineering work to be done, it is often worthwhile to separate it from short-term machine replacement and repair work. The division between central staff and local staff may be determined in this way, the central staff being concerned primarily with long-range activities. In sales, if the long-range product and merchandising planning function is not separated from the current sales research function, the current items get all the attention.

Pinpointing long-range responsibility may be especially important at the top level. Because a chief executive of a growing firm is constantly facing one current problem after another, it is difficult for him to sit back and do the long-range planning that he knows is necessary. As a consequence, the company does not grow soundly. Perhaps it fails to diversify. Gaps appear in functions, product lines, and programs. At that point it may be wise for a president to appoint an executive vice-president with a responsibility for supervising all operating functions and meeting all current problems. The president, in turn, could focus primarily on the long-range areas—of 5, 10, 15 years or more. He will be giving a considerable part of his time to planning, to long-range development, to corporate policy, and to working with the executive vice-president in coordinating current operations with the long-term plan. Such a setup, however, requires a very careful definition of function between the two men. It is apparent, of course, that there is bound to be some overlap. The president, however, must curb his natural tendency to become too involved in the current administrative problems. When carefully worked out, such an organizational setup is frequently highly advantageous, even in relatively small firms.

Define Limits for Staff Functions

It is increasingly important that the *limits for staff functions should be carefully defined as the firm grows* larger if these are not to encroach on supervisory functions of the line. As the number of staff functions increases, they may, in total, exercise such an influence on the line that the line cannot move for fear of violating some staff program. This fear is aggravated with central staff because they generally have the ear of top management.

In large companies particularly, central staff functions contribute to the firm primarily in the area of policy recommendations, in training local staff, and in developing the broad policies and procedures needed for company-wide control. Specific procedures should still be the sphere of the local staff or line. Even here, however, there is a tendency for central staff to exercise control through its policy function, either with conflicting policies or else with policies that in effect dictate procedures. It is especially important here to apply the "intent" approach to policy discussed in Chapter 6, page 59. Another way to control staff impact on the line is to combine as many staff functions as possible under a vice-president (perhaps the vice-president of administration). One effect of this vice-president setup is that it leaves the chief executive free to draw closer to his line functions. Too frequently there is a tendency for an executive to combine line (rather than staff) functions. As a fundamental rule of organization, it is our belief that *an executive* (or manager) *should organize to be as close as possible to his line functions.* The line accomplishes the basic work of the enterprise. If he must be separated from any individual functions, it is better that they be staff functions. He will usually develop a more virile and results-getting operation.

Central Staff vs. *Local Staff Functions*

Large institutions usually develop both central staff and local staff. The central staff is in the home office, with company-wide responsibility. The local staff works for a lower-level line manager in charge of a location, department, or division. There is a danger of duplication between the two, and in addition the danger that central staff will gradually override the local staff and local line even though central staff becomes removed from the everyday local problems. Local people then hesitate to take hard-hitting action. Maintaining virility in both staffs requires a new concept of operations on the part of the executive.

A related problem, but one that does not appear so on the surface, may occur in the case of a plant manager in a highly centralized firm. Such a plant manager may be expected to follow all the staff procedures of the central office, make sure he informs everybody soundly, and at the same time make a reasonable accomplishment in his plant. It may require a virtual superman to balance off all these requirements—one of the most effective arguments for decentralization. Contrary to general opinion, a completely centralized operation too frequently requires extraordinary ability in such a plant manager if he is to have a good accomplishment in the field and still satisfy all central office demands. The natural tendency is to simply follow the dictates of the central office without giving proper weight to the local requirements of operations. The fostering of a follow-directions attitude is one of the most debilitating effects of centralized operations. It is a strong deterrent to the development of the plant or branch manager out in the field, and, of course, in turn, to the development of all his subordinate supervisors.

Staff action is usually called for when line has problems on which staff may be able to help them. Usually a staff man on the scene is in closer tune with the ramifications of the problem. He tends to be more flexible in blending into line needs. A good over-all approach is to *have central staff do only what cannot be done locally*. As far as possible, everything that can be done locally should be delegated to the local staff; otherwise the central staff tends to run the local operation through detailed instructions. In actual practice, they are often too removed from the local problems to adequately control them anyway. There is constant pressure, however, for central staff to retain certain functions because these functions have some tenuous tie-in to other central activities in which they are engaged, even though the former could be carried out by local staff.

Ordinarily, central staff should develop and audit over-all policies and over-all procedures. They should assist local staff on research and on installation of their programs and should train local staff in the basic elements of their functions. The day-to-day operation should be left to local staff wherever possible. In reality, central staff are consultants. They should in most cases work themselves out of business. If they merely work themselves into more and more detailed control of local operations, it is likely that their basic setup is wrong. They probably have not analyzed the procedures and policies they propose in order to determine how far local staff may deviate before any serious company-wide problem develops.

Use of Management Committees

Management committees become quite prevalent early in the growth cycle of a firm. The chief executive occupies a lonely position. He likes to be assured that everyone is with him, so he organizes a management committee composed of his chief subordinates. Such a committee usually starts with a commendable desire to weigh all opinions on important decisions, but it can easily have a detrimental effect. Sometimes it merely multiplies the expression of inexpert opinion by giving voice to executives in areas with which they are unfamiliar. Good programs may, as a result, be retarded. Executives have strong vested interest in retaining their positions and may resist changes such as those which may result from an over-all organization plan. It is unlikely that all would agree on these proposed changes. Some would be bound to see in them a threat to their positions. Sometimes these committees see only the obstacles and overlook the creative aspects of a program. In addition, management committees may provide yet another way of avoiding accountability.

In most cases a management committee should not have the authority to make decisions. Its primary function should be that of an advisor to the chief, not a substitute for the chief in making decisions. It may also be used to inform people of important programs that may possibly affect their responsibilities. The information function must be carefully separated, however, from the recommendation function.

Management committees are usually most effective when the chairmanship changes with the problem to be considered, in line with the rule for selection of a committee chairman discussed in Chapter 11, page 138. When the subject under discussion is in the prime area of one of the members, he could be chairman and assume full responsibility for preparation of an agenda, for presenting data, for guiding the discussion, and for getting solutions and action. For example, if a sales problem is considered, the vice-president in charge of sales may run the meeting; if the topic is a control problem, the controller, and so on.

The chief executive is relieved of the burden of preparation, and the personal accountability that must always rest with the individual executive under the chief remains undiluted.

Otherwise the senior executive naturally tends to be the chairman of a committee, thereby encouraging an insidious trend toward nonaccountability on the part of the other executives as well as a general looseness in operation. The weakness is particularly evident when the committee is considering a "sticky" policy in the field of one of the members. That member may easily thereafter assume less personal accountability for the effectiveness of the policy.

DEVELOP A SOUND PATTERN OF DELEGATION

When many staff functions come into the picture, action down the line may be retarded because of poor delegation. There may be more stalemates than formerly, even though more experts are available. The experts may have been set up as a crutch for a poor line setup. The executive may then find it difficult to control operations, so he tends toward more central control, and then action moves even more slowly.

Staff to the Local Level

We have suggested that staff people should report to the lowest line level possible. This has special implications when considering the relationship between central and local staff. For example, in a branch plant local current engineering, local personnel, and local control should usually be handled by local men reporting directly to the local manager. They frequently make a more effective contribution under this setup. They are able to make quicker decisions, since they have more facts at hand, and tend to get more cooperation. They are usually held more accountable by results, because their immediate superior, the plant or branch manager, is very conscious of the results he wishes to achieve. The staff men grow better because they must solve the problems. An excessive growth of staff is less likely.

One objection made to this arrangement is that non-uniform staff operations may result, the presumption being, of course, that uniform staff operations are always advantageous. Very frequently they are not, but this is not recognized by central staff. There may be local conditions in one area that are far different from those in another. A local staff man would be much more sensitive to these. Where uniformity is vital, its necessity can be clearly stated in defining the relationship between the central and local staff.

We should emphasize that we recommend this setup, even though it means a break-up of responsibilities. For example, it may be that a company-wide salary administration program is advisable. Even so, local administration of this program may very well be handled by the local salary people. In other words, even where over-all coordination is necessary, there is nothing wrong with cutting off that part which could be locally administered and referring it to local staff. With broad policies as guides this is still highly desirable.

Two- or three-tier staff functions in the home office

should also be avoided. In our experience, the value of each of these levels decreases. The lower levels should be working on specific operating problems, which they will understand better if they are at the location where the problems are occurring. If you find it necessary to keep some of these people in the home office central staff, make sure that the lower-tier staff people who work on problems for local line are working directly with the local line people concerned, and not with the central line. To the extent that they work with the central line (as they would like to) they tend to be less effective and also to appear domineering to local line. The situation is complicated by the fact that they are usually quite junior to many line people they try to advise. They are also removed from the problems on which they are supposed to provide help.

In other words, if you do have a central staff function with several tiers, the lower people in this group should operate just as if they were local staff. They should work directly with the local people concerned and be measured by local accomplishment. You can readily see the difficulty of doing this in practice and therefore the wisdom of actually decentralizing and having these people report directly to local management. The central staff head naturally wishes to keep close control of their work. When he does, he tends to override local line people even on local adaptations that would not seriously affect over-all company operations.

Echelons in the Line

Although an executive should have his subordinates plan their own organization structure, he should be very concerned about the number of echelons in the line. The prime basis for communicating his policies and programs will be through these line echelons. Every time an extra level is added, the obstacles and difficulties of getting programs going are increased. Many executives are not concerned about the number of levels under them. They do not consider the echelons below the people reporting directly to them as their problem. *The number of levels in the line,* however, *should be kept to a minimum* if the executive wishes to get a hard-hitting, driving operation. Each level seems to reduce the effectiveness of communications (we feel about 25 per cent). An executive who experiences difficulties in communications will often devise an elaborate communications program to solve it. The problem may not be communications at all, but merely too many echelons between himself and the first-line supervisors. It is inevitable, then, that programs will not move.

Span of Control—Different Objectives

Supervision may be complex in another way. The work under an executive may need quite a variety of objectives in order to contribute soundly to over-all company objectives. This could be true even if the work is not dissimilar. An executive or manager must spend considerable care and time in working out these objectives and laying out methods for holding people accountable for them so that he arrives at balanced results—it takes time. For sound delegation *each group* being supervised *should be limited in the number of nonrelated objectives it has.* The manager can then delegate and control more easily.

Companies that diversify often face many unexpected setbacks because they assume that the new divisions are similar to the old. They do not take the time to think through the changes in objectives that are necessary for the new divisions and the ramifications of these changes as they affect staff functions and policy.

Span of Control—Effective Controls

A realistic control program that develops clear and timely interpretation for all management men is extremely important for stimulating sound management action in a complex enterprise. Unfortunately, as a firm grows in complexity, the record system also grows in complexity and, too frequently, in inadequacy. Reports are given very late, and they are merely over-all reports going up to the top, a broad history of operation. The inclination is increasingly to use "averages" for allocations. Responsibility accounting seems too difficult and cumbersome because of the size of the operation. As a consequence, men down the line do not learn to use records.

As we have said earlier, the record plan should be developed so that each management man gets information that will tell him how he is coming in regard to his objectives. If this reporting is done well, the number of men that a manager or executive can supervise directly will increase. Fewer supervisors or managers are necessary, yet good results may still be obtained. In addition, fewer echelons will be needed between the chief executive and the scene of operations, making it easier for him to coordinate the total operation.

18

Stimulating Cooperation in Complex Organizations

In multiple organizations the positions both of staff and of line must be very carefully defined so that they will cooperate and so that people take action. The environment becomes more political with company expansion and one man may try to outshine the other. Each has a responsibility, but they do not seem to blend well in actual operation. Because of the interweaving of responsibilities, special attention must be given to such areas as authority, account-ability, and tie-in controls.

AUTHORITY TIE-IN

The problem of giving staff authority increases as the company grows larger. Because staff is more removed from operations, they feel they need more authority in order to get compliance with their programs. However, such staff authority acts as a restriction on the authority of the line. Defining staff authority so the firm may capitalize on staff's expertness without excessive (and probably debilitating) restrictions on the line is a delicate problem.

Tying Central Staff to Local Staff

The division of authority between central staff and local staff must be carefully considered. The authority of central staff should, of course, be parallel with the general responsibilities that have been laid out for them. We have suggested that these should be in harmony with the over-all responsibilities retained by the central chief executive. Central staff should, therefore, have authority to propose company-wide policies, to audit broad procedures, and to see that the broad policies are being generally adhered to. This only applies to those policies that require company-wide uniformity! The same would be true of broad procedures. Otherwise the very operation of central staff tends to constrict the authority of line people to less than that intended by the chief executive. In a number of companies detailed auditing has centralized the operation in practice even though the chief executive felt he was operating on a decentralized basis. It is sometimes the reason why decentralization fails.

The local staff, in turn, should have the authority to determine the specific day-to-day application of procedures and should make the changes necessary to meet current conditions. One way for a chief executive to keep perspective on central staff is to recognize that *the scope of the central or local staff man should be roughly equivalent to the sphere of influence of the executive that he serves.* If the central line executive has delegated considerable autonomy to a local line executive, then the staff men serving that local line executive should have an equivalent autonomy in their areas of responsibility. An executive must cross-compare his delegations to his line and staff subordinates to be sure that their authority is consonant. If he does not, his staff delegation, in effect, limits the authority he felt he had delegated to his line subordinates. This cross comparison is an excellent way to approach decentralization of staff functions.

If the company has decentralized authority to division or branch operation, decentralized staff authority is automatic. The converse would also be true. It is impossible to decentralize staff authority unless you have first decentralized line authority. Many executives have been ensnared by a morass of central staff services because they have failed to realize this. As a consequence, men down the line fail to assume responsibility for their function and do not develop strong management insight.

An added point—the authority of local staff must have a margin for local error. It should be set in accordance with the error allowed the local manager. Requiring strict adherence to procedures set up by central staff with no allowance for local error generally leads to weak and ineffectual local staff (and local line). The net result is usually disappointing. One way to force this margin for local error is to require central staff to propose tolerances as a standard part of any policy or procedure that they propose. These give the chief executive a check on the centralizing action of central staff.

Broad Error with Broad Result

Central staff is set up primarily for broad policy and broad procedure development. A stumbling block is often the too narrow scope of the error permitted for them. If they are to leave current administration primarily to local staff, they must have enough leeway in authority so that broad local deviations are acceptable. Otherwise they are not encouraged to allow local staff to exercise their own judgment.

A chief executive often loses sight of the leeway that central staff must be allowed when he directs his central staff. It is easy to succumb to the temptation of expecting central staff to be on top of all details of local administration. On the contrary, it is essential that the executive make clear to a central staff officer the extent of the deviation that he would be permitted locally before incurring specific criticism. Failure to do so is often the reason why central staff tends toward a rigid control of even minor procedures in local operations. Considering that the chief executive expects central staff to be on top of all details, this is perfectly natural. The central staff concern about local detail is often attributed to the empire-building tendency of the central staff officer, but in many cases it merely reflects failure on the part of the chief executive to carefully delineate the breadth of authority (error tolerance) that he is permitting the central staff officer, including the allowable local staff deviation.

MAINTAIN PERSONAL ACCOUNTABILITY

Personal accountability tends to get lost when the operation becomes diversified. Staff seems to avoid accountability and to become more immersed in the techniques of their specialties. At the same time line managers can easily feel relieved of accountability, because staff is presumably working out all plans and numerous procedures are set up to be complied with. With the addition of many staff services this problem multiplies. It may be compounded by a failure to keep everyone steered in the same direction. It now becomes extremely difficult to coordinate pay, appraisals, and promotion systems at all levels to point both staff and line in the same direction—the direction of maximum accomplishment of company objectives. Procedures and protocol replace accountability.

Highlight Total Effect of the Function

It is comparatively easy to fall into the trap of emphasizing only part of a man's job. If you wish to maintain accountability at every level, a consistent attempt must be made to make each man personally accountable for the total effect of his function, and for the total cost. The executive must think through the ramifications of the function in order to trace its full effect. To do this, measurement is necessary, not vague comments such as, "It's good," or "People like it." The measurement system should reflect the effect of each key management man down the line. Otherwise it may be difficult to force accountability for the full impact of the job.

Since staff is set up as an auxiliary function to get added result from the line, the true results—or extra contribution of staff compared to its cost—should be measured as far as possible. Sometimes this can be done on a spot basis, at other times on a departmental comparison basis. In certain cases it may take a long period of time (perhaps several years).

In considering the accountability of staff, only the final result (to the point of efficient operation) should be considered. The measurement should get down to some improvement in line results. A measurement of staff activity as activity tends to be weak. In addition, the total cost should be consistent with the result.

For example, a design engineer who develops a product is often little concerned with the costs of producing the product. "That's production's job." Logical though it may seem, this attitude can lead to high production costs on new products. It is often advisable to make the engineer accountable for producing the product all the way through to the point where he proves in the first production run that it is feasible to produce it in the plant at a specific cost. All the cost of developing, experimenting, running pilot runs, and even perfecting production runs up to this point would be counted against the project. At first, this type of accountability may seem to be unfair to the development engineer. Through such accountability, however, he becomes really interested in the total cost to the company of product development and aware of the need for carefully thinking through the problems of the product in production before he begins to issue material or production specifications. In many cases the setup will be a very powerful influence for reducing both the cost of development and the cost of getting new products into production with few snags. At times the latter costs can be as great as the former. The development engineer, in turn, becomes a broader-gauge man, since he is now more sensitive to the impact of his specifications on production.

Give Double Credit

We mentioned in Chapter 16, page 200, that their is always overlap between staff and line; that there is never single accountability in staff—multiple accountability is implicit in the operation of staff. We cannot overemphasize the fact that staff (including central staff) must be given full credit for any accomplishment in its function. When staff is accountable for simply "advising" or "consulting with," as is so often true with central staff, this double recording is not usually done. All records should tie in to the final measurement of the accomplishment of the individual, even for central staff, though it is more difficult there. Better cooperation develops between central staff and the various other line and staff groups.

Triple Credit May Be Necessary

In applying the rule that each staff man must be accountable for his final effect on the line, you may allow triple credit at times. It may appear to be counter to most accounting principles, but if you wish to hold the staff people accountable for the objectives set up for them, it may be necessary. A triple-credit situation may be particularly necessary where central staff is involved (central staff, local staff, and line must all get credit).

If you find yourself faced with giving triple (or more) credit, it might, however, be an indication that you should question the staff setup, unless one of the persons is in a control recording function or a central staff function. The situation may highlight the fact that two functions aiming at the same result should be combined. It is easier to give credit if there is no need for individual staff functions to vie with each other for their share of the credit for accomplishment.

A good example of the advantages of combination occurs where you have a plant engineer, a maintenance foreman, and a production foreman. The production foreman is presumably held accountable in his unit cost objective for cost of machines. The maintenance foreman is accountable for cost of maintaining the machines. The plant engineer is accountable for the cost of buying machines that produce cheaply. Each, however, affects the other. It is often helpful to combine the job of plant engineer with that of maintenance engineer. One over-all staff accountability is then established for providing the lowest machine cost per unit and a more cooperative approach between maintenance and plant engineering often develops. The plant engineer becomes much more sensitive to the maintenance problems connected with any new machine installation he is contemplating. A similar combination may sometimes be profitably made of certain public relations and personnel positions (where community relations tied to plant operation is the principal public relations problem).

Staff Work through Reports

Many staff functions tend to do all their work through reports. Staffs who have to operate through reports alone are usually not very effective. It is difficult at best to influence people in this way, and most staff work requires a strong influence on the work of the line in order to get results that actually improve operations. Like supervisors, staff men are often only as effective as their face-to-face contacts allow—a general limitation on staff and a good rule of thumb to consider in deciding where to set up staff functions. It is also another reason for having them report to the lowest line level possible instead of building up a large central staff group.

Lead to Decentralization

As firms grow in size and complexity, there is a natural move toward centralization in order to get control. (Decentralization does not necessarily involve geography. It is really a process of giving maximum authority down the line.) The consequence is often insensitive decision making—insensitive to local problems. To counteract the difficulty a firm may decide to decentralize authority in order to give managers plenty of leeway. They may then be astonished at the increase in cost and in the number of new problems incurred and gravitate back to the refuge of centralized control. This cycle often occurs because they fail to realize that decentralization does not start with authority. It must start with accountability. No one should ever have authority until he has been made firmly accountable for the sound administration of his authority. Developing sound accountability requires careful planning. Failure to set up accountability first is a prime error in many decentralization programs and frequently leads to thousands of dollars of waste and extra cost in their early stages. It very often sours executives on the whole decentralization principle.

You can see that standardization makes decentralization easy because you can force accountability. It is easier to set sound objectives and to hold people accountable for them. This is why decentralized plant or office operations engaged in repetitive work generally seem to work satisfactorily—it is possible to force accountability without excessive home office pressure. The opposite may be true, however, where each branch has variable problems daily, as is the case in custom selling.

CONTROLS MUST REFLECT THE CENTRAL STAFF SETUP

As companies become more complex, there is unfortunately not a corresponding development in a system for recording the impact of staff, especially central staff. Because of the difficulty in precise measurement, there is a natural reluctance to attempt any measurement. As a consequence, staff has no personal accountability. The comment is made, "They can't be measured." In our experience, this is often not true. It is true, however, that measurement is often complicated and difficult—the infiltration of staff is harder to trace down than when the organization was simpler. There is, however, all the more reason why careful record systems should be devised to point up the success (or lack of it) of staff. Otherwise an executive will not know which staff functions to emphasize.

To start out, central staff must be charged with the total over-all effect of their function (both the results and the cost) down the line. A doubling up of credit, or discredit, with local staff is often advisable since one measurement of central staff is the summation of the results of all local staffs in their field. You can readily see that, for such measurement, the starting point is a recording of the results of local staff. In general, central staff results are longer-range, but, nevertheless, the results of central staff and local staff must fit together.

A major weakness of most record systems is that they provide no record of the operation of central staff, very often because central staff has no objectives. You can see here the necessity for having clear objectives for a job in order to develop a sound management control system. Without clear objectives a control system is almost an impossibility. There is no standard against which to measure. Records simply become records of activity and do not force accountability.

The same rules apply to keeping records on central staff as apply to those on local staff. Central staff should be notified of over-all problems in the light of their authority. There is a danger, however, of letting central staff be in on every little problem that occurs locally, thereby highlighting minor staff problems on the local level. Central staff will then naturally tend to get into these problems, taking away the feeling of authority of local staff. In the last analysis, central staff cannot closely supervise local staff anyway, though current recording approaches generally have not recognized this. The reporting of minor items to central staff or line has often reversed the trend toward decentralization as between the home office and the local office or department. The chief executive may be at fault in expecting his central staff or line officers to be able to answer questions on minor details in the field. The chief executive must recognize these minor local deviations as part of the normal deviation or tolerance allowed central staff.

19

The Future of Management

THE MANAGEMENT of the future must provide the answer to the constant enigma of providing a full, challenging life while integrating rapid technological change into a dynamic society.

Technological improvement, better communications systems, and faster transportation facilities have all increased the complexity of enterprise. Improvements in standards of living now support a higher general level of education. The higher social demands of an educated electorate add to the complexity. As a consequence, governmental activities have become more extensive, both for the satisfaction of the wants of the citizenry and for the better control of complex industrial enterprises for the good of the group. Both in manufacturing and in record systems automation has made operations more intricate, requiring large capital expenditures for machine installations which require intricate management balancing to capitalize on them. It appears that these conditions will have a greater rather than a lesser impact in the future, requiring an even more sophisticated approach to the management of an enterprise.

Although this increasing complexity in operations seems inevitable, the basic problem of management is still that of maintaining the essential simplicity in principle that exists when an enterprise consists of merely a supervisor and one subordinate. It is the responsibility of management to continue to give attention to the accomplishment of the individual at the same time that it integrates the individual accomplishments of all, even in the most complex enterprise. This is essentially a problem of analyzing intricate relationships and difficult, integrated timing requirements.

As an enterprise becomes more complex, there is an understandable inclination to reduce all relationships to automatic procedures. This inclination carries over to the management of people, as is often indicated by the statement that they (the employees) "ought" to act a certain way. However, people are thinking, feeling individuals and do not readily conform to a robotistic mold. Even in the most complicated enterprise management must still get back to basics. First, the expected result should be defined for every individual so that he knows where he stands and is steered in the direction of the objectives of the enterprise. Second, individuals must still have the maximum leeway in which to exercise their initiative and ingenuity if management is to fully capitalize on the abilities of its people. In effect, large organizations must combat the natural centralization that creeps in through policies, budgets, procedures, and cost control, a centralization which inevitably leads to a lesser return from the individual and to the strapping and the retarding of his growth. Third, the intricate web of accountability must be worked out so that each individual maintains a sense of personal obligation for his share of the accomplishment of the total accomplishment of the enterprise. Only then can strength be maintained throughout the enterprise. Finally, the record system must be designed to give every individual significant information so that he may take appropriate action.

To meet the problems of more complex enterprise, the whole management climate must be studied from the point of view of the individual as he fits into the enterprise. His personal needs and satisfactions must be appropriately blended with the needs of the enterprise. In short, the greatest achievement will come from the expansion of the individual, his abilities and personality. Basically, then, management must develop as broad a horizon as possible for every position, with guideposts along the way rather than rigid fences that hem the individual into a completely preplanned industrial existence.

Such a management design offers a great opportunity to any society to accomplish the greatest possible good from the technological advances made in all fields. It provides any enterprise with the basis for keeping pace with all new types of knowledge and assimilating them profitably into the mechanics of the enterprise. Each enterprise and industry as a whole will be much better able to leapfrog forward whenever new breakthroughs occur in any particular science or segment of a science. Only management can provide a basis for fully and swiftly capitalizing on the technological achievements of the various sciences.

More important, society will profit by the much greater breadth in the development of each individual. Each individual will cultivate his abilities more fully—often abilities which he did not even know he had. Each man is therefore made more complete, in that he is better able to nurture dormant abilities to a flowering that will maximize his total impact on problems that he faces.

In the process each individual will develop a broader sense of responsibility in addition to a heightened sense of achievement. Each citizen will, therefore, cultivate a greater degree of self-reliance, providing a sound basis for strong and responsible citizenship—a requirement if democracy is to be a vibrant fact rather than a philosophical fiction. The necessity for such a development grows more critical as societies become more complex in that a broader responsibility must finally reside in each individual citizen, particularly as increased educational opportunities are provided for more and more people. In essence, men will grow as individuals along with their growth in academic learning.

In the last analysis the strength or weakness of a democracy rests on the strengths or weaknesses of its individual citizens. The difficulties in meeting changing conditions can only be met by an enlightened and responsible citizenry; otherwise rigidity sets in. Special-interest groups attain undue influence and the flexibility needed for obtaining quick, incisive action may be lost.

This development of the individual, along with an almost fantastic capitalization on technological improvements as they continue to mushroom, is the true mission of the management of the future. These goals can be fully achieved only through the development and application of farsighted management principles in the coordinating of enterprise. One of the greatest challenges of a society is that presented to management in making practical sense out of an increasing whirl of technological change. It will remain for many years to come the constant frontier, and become even more demanding as technology and society change further. Man must manage change and complexity or else they will manage man, with the inevitable collapse of civilized society.

Index